BLAMELESS

Lessons for today
from the Book of Job

Richard Graham-Taylor

Quine & Cubbon Ltd.
Athol Street
Port St. Mary
Isle of Man
IM9 5DS

ISBN: 1 903725 03 8

Preamble

Why do bad things happen to good people? Where is God when you really need Him? Why is the purpose and pattern of life so baffling at times? What is really going on in the world? Can any of us know for sure? Do our leaders have a clue what they're doing and where they're taking us? Who's to blame for the mess we're in?

Are these the kind of questions you are asking yourself? Looking at the daily newspapers it seems the blind are leading the blind. Just because we are so scientifically clever and techno brilliant is no good reason to think we can now do without God to guide us. In fact, the more knowledge we acquire the more reason we have to seek God's wisdom in how to apply it properly.

The Book of Job may seem to some like an odd place to look for answers. At first glance it appears to be an unlikely story with no clear-cut message. Job suffers outrageous misfortune at the hands of the devil, who has been put up to his tricks by God Himself. But this book asks the questions that philosophers and theologians have pondered throughout history. Why are we here? What is life all about? Why do good folk suffer? Where does God fit in? How is He involved, and if so, where's the justice in it all?

As one immerses oneself in the narrative and the discourses, light starts dawning and gradually answers begin to take shape. It is fascinating to see how divine wisdom unveils these spiritual mysteries letting us glimpse God's viewpoint and observe things from His perspective.

Without doubt a better acquaintance with and understanding of Job is vital for the church today – especially as the signs indicating the approach of the end-times are becoming more pronounced and insistent. Christians will be having to face some tough times and will need to develop all the integrity and understanding they can before it is too late. Perseverance, patience and longsuffering are all attributes we will need in full measure as the countdown begins. Job is the biblical epitome of these characteristics. What's more, the epistle of James reminds us, "You too, be patient and stand firm, because the Lord's coming is near.......... The Judge is standing at the door! Brothers, as an example of patience in the face of suffering, take the prophets who spoke in the name of the Lord. As you know we consider blessed those who have persevered. You have heard of Job's perseverance and have seen what the Lord finally brought about. The Lord is full of compassion and mercy."

Teaching along these lines is not so popular in these pleasure and leisure loving days. But it is nonetheless truth – and we ignore it at our peril. How many Christians are still camping beside dried up streams which once flowed with rivers of living water, because they grew too comfy and cosy and turned a deaf ear and blind eye to God's beckoning to move onwards and upwards to greater and better things. Doing good is good, but doing better is better. We all need to beware of complacency. Are we relying on the supply or the supplier? This is the true test of a Christian. It was the test that Job was put through, and we can learn valuable lessons from his experience.

I have written this book in an expository fashion. At the head of each chapter I have indicated the portion of the Book of Job being dealt with. I have then paraphrased in modern vernacular the conversations that take place. Purists may wince, but I think the points being made hit home much more tellingly. This has also enabled me to cut down on the archaically mannered verbosity. For instance, when Elihu introduces himself into the fray he takes more than a chapter making introductory remarks, such as, 'I too will have my say; I too will tell what I know. For I am full of words (you can say that again!), and the spirit within compels me; inside I am like bottled up wine bursting to gush forth. I must speak and find relief; I must open my lips and reply. Listen to my words, pay attention to everything I say. I am about to open my mouth; my words are on the tip of my tongue.' A little irreverently this reminds me of a small boy desperately crossing and uncrossing his legs as he waits impatiently in a queue for the loo! By-passing verses like these, to my mind, keeps the debate in sharper focus, although I am well aware of what Revelation 22v19 has to say on the subject of biblical editing! With the exception of this and similar short-cuts, I have followed the exact sequence of the discourses and the development of the various philosophical and theological arguments with appropriate comment from time to time prompted by the text.

I feel very strongly that the nub and the hub of this book is to be found at the end of chapter 10. God is speaking to this generation of Christians to cling on to Him a lot more tightly than we are presently in the habit of doing. If we don't demonstrate to the world at large that we believe it is in Him alone 'we live and move and have our being', why should anyone else believe it?

I would like to dedicate this book to my daughter, Oona, who has so painstakingly and perseveringly – might I say, 'in Job-like fashion'! – done the proof-reading and to my friends, Mike Bowerman and George Manderson in the Cayman Islands, for their encouragement. As a result of all the time I have spent meditating on the Book of Job whilst writing these pages much was revealed to me that previously I had only seen through a glass darkly; so I am hopeful that readers will be led to a clearer understanding of God's point of view when it comes to finding answers to the questions I posed in the opening paragraph. It is after all the mind of Christ we must all endeavour to aspire to.

Right now the finger of God is pointing at us. It is senseless for us to be shaking our fists back at Him. Ever since the Garden of Eden man has been trying to find someone else to blame for his shortcomings. Blamelessness is found only in Jesus Christ, nailed to the Cross, triumphantly resurrected and gloriously ascended into heaven. That, in a nutshell, is mankind's only hope of salvation in today's crazy world.

R M G Graham-Taylor

1 Ravenscliffe Mews
Douglas, Isle of Man
IM1 5BN

Contents

Page

Preamble   3

Chapter 1   Job Who?   10

Chapter 2   Meet The Family!   17

Chapter 3   The Plot Thickens   25

Chapter 4   Job's Second Test   31

Chapter 5   The Coming of the Comforters   38

Chapter 6   Job and Bildad   46

Chapter 7   Zophar - so good!   53

Chapter 8   I Know That My Redeemer Lives   59

Chapter 9   The Discomforters!   65

Chapter 10   My God, My God, Why Have You Forsaken Me?   72

Chapter 11   Young Elihu   85

Chapter 12   God Inhabits The Praises Of His People   91

Chapter 13   The Lord Speaks   97

Chapter 14   Dinosaurs and Dragons   106

Chapter 15   The End Of The Matter   114

Epilogue   121

Chapter 1

Job Who?

"In the land of Uz there lived a man whose name was Job."

Thus begins the Book of Job. Where on earth is Uz? There has been much scholarly speculation leaving no one very sure. I am a firm believer that the Bible is its own best interpreter. Uz is mentioned in Genesis 10:23 as being one of the sons of Aram, who in turn was a son of Shem of Noah's Ark fame. Now we not only have an approximate location for Uz, but also some idea as to when Job lived. Tribal lands used to take their names from their patriarchal founding fathers. So the land of Uz was probably a district within the territory of Aram and the Arameans, whose language was Aramaic, which was still widely spoken in the Holy Land in Jesus' time.

According to biblical chronology, the flood occurred around 3000 B.C. What with the kind of ages people lived to in those days, the tribe and land of Uz would have very likely come into existence no later than 2500 B.C. inhabiting a region somewhere in the foothills of what is today the uplands of northern Syria and Iraq. Possibly not that far from the notorious Tower of Babel. With the flood still a vivid memory folk were understandably reluctant to populate the fertile lowland plains of Mesopotamia despite the fact that God had promised never to repeat the performance. What an unbelieving bunch we are!

It's not unlike when Moses was explaining to the Israelites how God would supply them with manna in the wilderness every morning before breakfast. He told them to gather just enough for the day. No overloading the shopping trolley or stockpiling allowed. Needless to say some paid no attention and what they had squirreled away went rotten and maggoty overnight. Then again, they were told to pick up a double portion on Friday to enable them to stay at home and rest up on the Sabbath. God said there would be no manna on the ground on Saturday mornings. Sure enough, the Bible tells us some went out with their shopping baskets that very day regardless, but found nothing!

About 600 years on from the foundation of Uz a direct descendant of Shem turns up on the scene who is none other than old father Abraham, living there or thereabouts and still speaking Aramaic. It was he who heard the call of God and emigrated to the land of Canaan. He made a fortune as many émigrés so often do, and founded a dynasty. His younger son, Isaac, inherited the family business, whilst the elder, Ishmael, set off eastward into what would now be Jordan, and did pretty well for himself too. After Abraham's wife, Sarah, died he married a lady called Keturah and had a number of children by her who also all wandered off in an easterly direction. One of her grandsons was a fellow by the name of Bildad, of whom we shall assuredly hear more later.

Isaac married a girl from way back home in Aram, who also happened to be his cousin, and she produced twins, Esau and Jacob. Once again the younger son, Jacob, took over the family business, whilst the elder pushed off east to seek his fame and fortune in modern day south Jordan, founding a country called Edom. He had a son named Eliphaz, the Temanite, who plays a major role in our unfolding drama. Interestingly, Teman, some 1,000 years later, as mentioned in Jeremiah 49:7, had become a by-word for wisdom and prudence.

Jacob, like his father and grandfather before him, found a wife – actually two wives (and a couple of concubines into the bargain!) – who were his relatives from the territory of Aram, and proceeded to have twelve sons and a daughter. It was this group, with their grandchildren and others, who eventually decided to up sticks in Canaan and go down and settle in Egypt where one of the sons, Joseph, had miraculously become prime minister. But that's another story.

I have laboured this genealogy somewhat to show how the pieces of the puzzle fit together. Abraham, Isaac, Jacob and his progeny represent the chosen people of God – the start of the Messianic family tree. Ishmael, Esau and their descendants are types of unsaved worldly wise men – the bootstrap religionists who believe a saviour is unnecessary because they think they can largely do it all by dint of their own wit and will.

Job, living in the land of Uz, was a grandson of Jacob. He had originally travelled down as a young boy with the rest of them into Egypt. His father was Issachar, and it is surely no coincidence, with an ancestor like Job, that the men of Issachar in King David's day had acquired the reputation of being a pretty wise and canny clan, being described in 1 Chronicles 12:32 as men who understood the times and knew what Israel should do. Coincidentally, one of the meanings in Hebrew for Job is 'the returning one'. This could clearly relate to his leaving Egypt and going back to his roots in Uz at some time before the going got rough and the Israelites found themselves enslaved to a 'pharoah who knew not Joseph'. This would have been about 1500 B.C.

To complete the dramatis personae we have Zophar, the Naamathite. His antecedents are rather more obscure, but it is generally thought that he was also an Edomite and consequently a close kinsman to Eliphaz. Finally there is

Elihu, the Buzite, indicating that he lived in the territory of Aram like Job. They may well have been close neighbours. Interestingly he is said to be a relative of Ram, the great grandson of Judah. He was therefore two generations younger than Job, but nonetheless a cousin, albeit twice removed. More significantly, he was an Israelite and an heir of the Abrahamic promise.

All of the characters are connected to Abraham in one way or another, but only Job and Elihu are in the direct line of 'promise' which runs through Isaac and Jacob. Genesis 12v3 tells us of God's promise that through this Messianic line all people on earth will be blessed. We need to bear in mind that at this point in time God's unfolding revelation of himself to mankind had only reached the fourth dispensation. There was 'innocence' in the Garden of Eden. Then 'conscience' at the time of the fall, followed by 'human government' when Noah, on behalf of all mankind, was effectively given the leasehold deeds to the earth and told to get on with populating and subduing it. With Abraham came the revelation that a right relationship with God can only be attained by faith and unwavering trust in His promises.

Many scholars would have us believe that the Book of Job is fiction. I beg to disagree. Job and his so-called comforters were real flesh and blood historical characters identifiable in the scriptures as we have seen. What happened at the time was probably not recorded immediately, but passed down from generation to generation as part of the oral tradition of the area. When finally written down it was inspired by God and can therefore be relied upon as true in all the essential details. God is not in the business of trying to hoodwink or deceive anyone. Quite the contrary in fact. Curiously there is no mention of, or any allusion to, the Exodus or Mosaic law throughout the narrative, which would support the view that the events must have taken place prior to 1300 B.C.

It is inconceivable that such foundation stones of the Jewish faith could be so totally ignored in an epic of this dimension had they already occurred. This is what makes Job's arguments with his friends about God 3,500 years ago so absolutely fascinating. It is here we will find the germ of all ancient comparative world religions – Judeo-Christian, Hindu, Buddhist, Jainism, Confucianism, and the rest.

Paleontology leads us to believe that people living in neolithic and bronze age times were almost sub-human, dressed in rags, living in caves and most likely hairy and unwashed. On the contrary, late stone age man was weaving fancy cloth to clothe himself, manufacturing beautifully decorated pottery, crafting high quality woodwork for houses, furniture and many sophisticated implements and constructing stone edifices that would put many a modern day builder to shame. In the year 1500

B.C. or thereabouts Job and his pals were not necessarily tent dwelling nomads, but could well have been living in stately pleasure domes and the lap of luxury even by today's standards.

Modern twenty-first century man has developed a peculiar arrogance which allows him to imagine that anyone living three or four thousand years ago must have been semi-moronic and totally uncultured, in a word a savage. Such notions could hardly be further from the truth. If Job were to visit Earth today he would doubtless consider us to be the barbarians. Despite all our wonderful technological inventions, we are very certainly no more intelligent, but, worse still, we are probably not half as wise – in a godly sense.

Chapter 2

Meet The Family!

(Job 1vv1 − 5)

Job was blameless and upright; he feared God and shunned evil. He had seven sons and three daughters, owned 7,000 sheep, 3,000 camels, 1,000 oxen, 500 donkeys, and had a large number of servants. He was the greatest man among all the people of the East.

We're looking here at a guy who's multi-mega-rich - a really high net worth individual. Sheep don't come cheap, and I have it on good authority that the going rate for racing camels is somewhere in the region of £50,000 a throw. Job's were probably not the thoroughbred variety, nonetheless they'd fetch a bob or two at market, as would 500 yoke of oxen and all those donkeys. He had a grown up family. His seven sons had all left home. They had their own places now where they seemed to be well provided for living a life of ease and pleasure, most likely on the settlements their father had made over to each of them.

Significantly we are told that he was blameless and upright, and he feared God and shunned evil. He is in fact held up as a paragon in the Book of Ezekiel as one of the three most noteworthy righteous men ever to have lived – the other two being Noah and Daniel. Odd isn't it that neither Abraham nor Moses gets a mention!

In Proverbs we read, "The fear of the Lord is the beginning of wisdom." Nowadays we have expressions such as, "That'll put the fear of God into him!" when referring to shock tactics or threats to gain an advantage over someone and to leave them quaking in their boots. This, I rather think, has more to do with the devil than with God. Being fearful of God today seems to many simply superstitious nonsense. After all, doesn't the New Testament tell us that God is love, and full of compassion and great mercy? Yes indeed. We are now living in the dispensation of 'grace' – God's unmerited favour towards us. He invites us all to accept adoption into his family. He wants to be our father and us to be his sons and daughters. As a result, Christian teaching has majored on the love of God and almost totally forgotten about the 'fear of the Lord'.

Because Job feared the Lord, it was God who set his life's agenda. He worried like any good and responsible dad when his sons and daughters were at their partying – eating and drinking and having a high old time – and let me tell you, we in the modern western world are mere ingénues when it comes to hospitality as practised by the ancient middle-easterners! In the Book of Esther we are told that King Xerxes opened up his palace to his guests for six months, topping it all off with a banquet where the wine flowed freely for seven days non-stop. There must have been some sore heads and bleary eyes after that!

Whilst on the subject of 'The Fear of God', it is interesting to note how many times it is recounted in the gospels that the disciples were afraid of 'gentle Jesus meek and mild'. When they saw Him walking on the water they were literally terrified until He called out to them not to be afraid. When He exorcised the demon possessed man and the herd of pigs rushed over the cliff and drowned in the lake, the people were scared out of their wits and begged Him to go away and leave them alone. Another time, Jesus was trying to explain to them about His death and resurrection. The disciples just couldn't grasp what it was He was telling them, but they were afraid to ask Him. Then when He commanded the winds and the waves to be still, they were filled with holy dread at such an awesome display of power. "Who is this bloke?" they wondered in fear and amazement.

To come face to face with unadulterated holiness is a pretty shattering experience for your average seven days-a-week sinner! Modern religious doctrine tries not to bother us unduly with things that make us feel so distinctly uncomfortable. In Job's day they would have had no trouble with this concept. Shem, who had been in the Ark with Noah, lived for 500 years after the flood subsided and would have been passing on an eye-witness account of what it had been like down to not far short of Abraham's time. Fascinatingly, old father Abraham was a mere ten generations removed from Shem, who quite possibly died, according to biblical chronology, during the patriarch's lifetime. To put this in perspective, it would be like someone living today who had met and spoken with Shakespeare or even Henry VIII. To these ancient worthies God's direct intervention in the affairs of mankind was recent history. At one fell swoop he had wiped all but eight people clean off the face of the earth because of their wickedness. This was a God you didn't want to mess with! To be fearful of Him was simple commonsense – and this is where we came in: "The fear of the Lord is the beginning of wisdom".

We are told that Job was 'blameless and upright'. Indeed a few paragraphs further on God is reported as saying, "There is no one on earth like him." These are impressive credentials. What does it mean to be 'blameless and upright'? Surely no human being can be that good? Doesn't scripture tell us that all have sinned and fallen short of the glory of God? In that case Job must have been a sinner just like the rest of us. So what was it that made him so special? As we delve deeper into Job's story all will be revealed.

For the moment let's continue to acquaint ourselves with the family. As already mentioned, Job's sons were real party animals entertaining one another in such lavish fashion that the feasting would sometimes continue for days. It seems that old man Job did not attend these sumptuous affairs, but stayed at home worrying about what his kids might be getting up to, praying all the while that God would protect them and see they came to no harm – just like many an anxious parent today. Times haven't changed much in 3,500 years, have they?

Here it is important to notice what he was thinking. "Perhaps my children have sinned and cursed God in their hearts." Between cursing God and blaspheming there is precious little difference. Throughout scripture we are constantly warned that the one thing that will get us into more trouble than practically anything else is blasphemy – taking the name of God in vain, as the third commandment puts it. In the New Testament Jesus said blasphemy against the Holy Spirit was an unforgivable sin. Yet hardly a day goes by without every one of us hearing blasphemy in one form or another. Job knew something that many of us would do well to re-learn and fast. God will not be mocked. He is not to be taken lightly. He is for real, big time, and certainly not to be trifled with if you know what's good for you. Now this is where the church today seems to have slipped up badly. They don't mind if their members snooze in the pews just so long as their names appear on the parish electoral roll. To God that kind of pseudo-Christian makes Him want to throw up.

I heard a preacher ask a congregation what they thought was the opposite of 'love'. Almost without thinking they replied, "Hate." "I don't agree," the preacher said, "In God's eyes, I think the opposite of 'love' is 'indifference'." I'm inclined to think he had a good point. 'Love' and 'hate' are very close to one another on the Richter scale of emotions. 'Indifference' would be at the other end of the thermometer. Scripture supports this, not only with the famous 'lukewarm' quote in Revelation 3:16, but also in Jeremiah 3:11 where the Lord tells the prophet that faithless Israel is more righteous than unfaithful Judah. What He is implying is that He'd rather be doing business with honest to goodness unbelievers than with unenthusiastic hypocritical Christians who are more of a hindrance than a help in getting the good news of the Kingdom spread abroad.

But I digress. We left Job on his knees before the Lord pleading God's mercy for his children. There were no mighty multinational insurance companies in Job's time where he could buy protection for himself, his family, and all his considerable possessions. Had that been the case, when the Sabeans and Chaldeans made off with his flocks and herds, all that would be necessary would be to put in a claim, go to market and start over. Similarly, when he got sick, a quick call to his private health providers and all would be taken care of. I am in no way advocating that we should not carry insurance on our cars and houses. In modern society that would, in many cases, be illegal anyway. The point I am making is, in order to understand Job's mindset, we need to picture ourselves in his position.

A good deal of the confidence we have in life as we go about our daily grind comes from the fact that there is a police force maintaining law and order, and there are various other social mechanisms in play to allow us to come and go in a reasonably peaceful fashion. This was not so with Job. Might was right in his day and you only owned what you and your friends could successfully defend. Plainly there are limits to what we puny humans can do in this respect. Hence the constant need to invoke the assistance of an all-powerful and all-seeing God as our shield and defender.

You wouldn't want to get into God's bad books and risk having His hedge of protection removed. Word passed down through the ages said that God liked sacrifices – particularly of livestock. Apparently He liked the aroma of the burning carcass. One wonders what He thought of the foot and mouth hecatombs across the English countryside in 2001 wafting their sickly 'sweet smelling savour' heavenward. Not much, is my guess. Diseased or crippled animals were specifically proscribed from the ancient sacrificial rituals.

So Job was a conscientious dad and devout believer in an

Almighty God whom all would do well to recognise and obey. But here is the interesting bit which 21st century man has lost sight of. If you believe in God, then He is the only one you can and must worship, regardless. Whether things are going well or taking a turn for the worse, there is literally no one else worthy of our worship. He is ultimately the only one who has the power to make a difference. There will be times when we are close to despair, but faith in an omnipotent, omniscient, omnipresent God convinces us that all is not lost because the God we believe in does, in the final analysis, have our best interests at heart. Hope springs eternal in the human breast. Once hope has gone then all hell breaks loose.

Chapter 3

The Plot Thickens

(Job 1vv6 – 22)

Whilst Job was humbly and dutifully getting on with being 'blameless and upright' something peculiar was happening in heaven. The angels came to present themselves before the Lord – and Satan also came with them. Now that in itself is strange indeed. The Bible tells us that Satan and his cohorts mounted a rebellion against God in heaven, were defeated, and thrown out. Thereafter they inhabited the spiritual realm on the earth creating all sorts of mischief and mayhem in the process. So where was this meeting taking place? Satan is banished from heaven, but God is free to go wherever he wishes – that is one of the privileges of being God! He is omnipresent after all!

A little heavenly logistics may now be helpful. The Bible speaks of three heavens. The first is the physical universe – the sky and the stars. The second is what Paul alludes to in Ephesians 6:12 when he mentions "the spiritual forces of evil in the heavenly realms." The third, also known as Paradise, is the place referred to in the Lord's Prayer when we say, "Thy will be done on earth as it is in heaven." Some may be wondering about the expression – the seventh heaven. The Old Testament has seven different designations for heaven; the seventh being "araboth" which is where the angels, the souls of the righteous, and all goodness reside. This equates with what Paul calls the third heaven in the New Testament.

Plainly God's meeting with Satan took place in the heavenly realms of the second heaven.

The Lord said to Satan, "What mischief have you been up to?"

Satan replied, "Oh, just the usual. You know the kind of things I'm good at. A bit of temptation here, a bit of sickness there and generally spreading as much misery around as I can, just to test this creation of yours to see if it really is able to withstand the stress and pressure you claim it can. One of these days I'll find a flaw in your plan. Then you won't be so 'God Almighty' any longer. You just wait and see!"

Satan glares defiantly at God with undisguised flames of hatred and envy flashing from his eyes.

Totally unperturbed, the Lord says, "By the way, have you seen my friend, Job, lately? Now, there's someone who's worth pitting your wits against if you want a real challenge. In my book he's blameless and upright. He fears me and will have nothing to do with you."

"Oh, yeah!" says the devil, "Why do you think Job fears you? He's got enough sense to know which side his bread is buttered. Because he prays regularly you've been protecting him and helped him to prosper. He's got it made. Anyone with his kind of good fortune is bound to be on your side. Let him suffer a little. Drag him through the bankruptcy courts. Let him see what it's like below the poverty line wondering where his next crust of bread is coming from. Then you'll soon discover his blamelessness and uprightness is a mere charade. Your much vaunted 'mankind' – made in your image! What a joke! That bunch of no-hopers will never be capable of anything more than cupboard love. You made them lower than the angels and that's where they'll always be."

Then the Lord said to Satan, "Very well then, I'll withdraw my protection from Job's family and possessions and let you do your damnedest. I don't believe it will make a blind bit of difference to his faith in Me. I know the heart of the man. His integrity is not dependent upon his external circumstances. Just you wait and see. I created mankind for better things than you will ever credit."

So off goes the devil on his fiendish mission. Down through history it has always been thus. Satan is dedicated to trying to prove God wrong. Why do you think so many are so frantically exercised in finding fault with the Bible? I don't see folk getting that worked up about the world's other holy writings. As far as Satan is concerned they are no problem. It's the Bible, and especially Jesus Christ, that gets him really riled. They are "Truth" and that is one thing he cannot abide. Jesus called him the father of lies. Deception is the name of his game.

Satan lost no time in dishing out his devilment. The roof fell in on Job's pleasant world. Talk about a stock market crash! His property and possessions were plundered by bandits and all his children killed in a freak storm. He was left with nothing. In modern parlance, he was ruined. He had gone from riches to rags in the blink of an eye.

Understandably Job was a tad more than a little distressed, and as was the custom in those days when disaster befell he tore his robes, shaved his head and tossed dust on himself as outward signs of his abject misery. But it's what he does next that shows the true character of the man. For a guy who had invested a great deal of effort to keep sweet with God, praying regularly for His protection, particularly on behalf of his kids, it would figure if he now felt a bit miffed that all that praying had been to no avail.

"God, where were you when all this was happening? If you're almighty, surely you could have prevented it?"

Isn't that the cry of so many whenever a calamity occurs? Here's where we see why God had called Job 'blameless'. Instead of blaming God he falls to the ground in worship and says: "Naked I came from my mother's womb, and naked I shall depart. The Lord gave and the Lord has taken away; blessed be the name of the Lord." It never entered Job's head to blame God for his misfortunes. How differently the world reacts today. We live in a culture of blame. Whenever something goes wrong we cast around for someone at whom we can point a finger. We sue and seek compensation and end up trusting no one – least of all, God. What a diabolically cunning plan the devil has devised to separate us from the love of God!

Now, many of you may be thinking that it is pathetically wimpish to sit back and not get riled when misfortune strikes – and I would agree. What is important is to have our anger pointed in the right direction. Never doubt that God loves us and always has our long term best interests at heart. We may not be able to understand what is going on, like Job, but there is never any mileage to be had from blaming God. He undoubtedly moves in mysterious ways His wonders to perform, but He is God and good will always be the eventual outcome, even if we cannot see it at this point in time. It is the world, the flesh and the devil that are the culprits. So, to be upright and blameless like Job, we need to take a good hard look at the way he reacted to his circumstances.

Stone-age Job was not such a savage after all! He knew a thing or two about wisdom and integrity that most folk today have completely forgotten. He had an unshakeable belief that God was all He claimed to be, come what may. Regardless of the weather his faith was unchangeable. Just like the ancient martyr, Polycarp, who when arrested at the age of 86 and ordered to deny Christ on pain of death famously said, "My Lord has been faithful to me all my life, how can I possibly be unfaithful to Him now?"

It is that kind of total commitment that seems to be so sadly lacking in the Christian faith we see practised today. Regrettably, the suicide bombers are perhaps the nearest equivalent we find in this generation of people prepared to give their all for a cause. Whilst on the subject, I suppose the Palestinians/Philistines could claim that the Israelis started this awful ball rolling, what with Samson's last hurrah, when he toppled the temple of Dagon killing, along with himself, three thousand in the process. This incidentally is slightly more than the number lost in the September 11th 2001 felling of the twin towers in New York. But I digress. Christian martyrdom is neither suicidal nor vindictive. It springs from the unwavering conviction that God's love will never fail. This is the uprightness and blamelessness of Job that so pleased his Maker.

Chapter 4

Job's Second Test

(Job 2vv1-10)

You'd think that poor old Job had suffered enough not to be put through the wringer again, wouldn't you? But he was about to discover that disasters can be a bit like number nine buses. None appear for seemingly ages then suddenly a whole herd bear down upon you! God was really pleased with the way Job had handled himself in the first test and mentioned as much to the devil.

"You've done your damnedest and Job's faith is still as solid as a rock. I told you there was no one on earth like him. He is blameless and upright, he fears me, and despite all the awful things you persuaded me to let you do to him he has still maintained his integrity. I rest my case," says God.

"Not so fast," retorts Satan truculently, "your pal Job may have lost all his outward trappings and trimmings, but he's still got his health. Let me take that away from him and then you'll soon see how fragile is that much vaunted faith of his. It won't be long before he starts cursing you to your face. This puny mankind of yours will give anything to save its skin. Just you wait and see!" He spat the challenge out venomously and waited defiantly to hear what God's response might be. He always found the Lord's unruffled equanimity whenever they had these exchanges so utterly infuriating.

"Oh," says God, "so you want another innings with Job, do you? I thought you'd already given him a pretty serious duffing up. You'll be wasting your time, but if you must, I will step aside and let you try your diabolics once more."

One thing you can be sure about the devil, he never stops trying. In fact he is extremely trying! So off he goes and sees to it that poor old Job gets desperately sick and breaks out in unsightly and painful sores all over his body. So wretched is his condition that even his wife turns on him and tells him it is about time he found another god who would take better care of him. "So much for all your integrity!" She moans, "This God you keep talking about and praying to doesn't seem to be bringing us much luck. Quite frankly you'd be better off dead!"

"Hush your mouth now, woman," says Job, "You're talking foolishness. We've had some mighty good times. You can't surely have forgotten those so soon? Now we've got a bad patch to go through. We can't expect blue skies

every day. This is when our integrity really gets tested."
Like the old hymn puts it:

"Not forever in green pastures

"would I ask my way to be,

"But the rough and rugged pathway

"would I tread rejoicingly."

Once again we are told that in all this Job did not sin. Here is an object lesson in how to face adversity. His response to calamity is much the same as that of the prophet, Habakkuk, who forecast the oncoming Babylonian conquest of Judah in about 600 BC along with all the accompanying distress and hardship. "Though the fig tree does not bud and there are no grapes on the vines, though the olive crop fails and the fields produce no food, though there are no sheep in the pen, no cattle in the stalls and the stock market falls, **YET I WILL REJOICE IN THE LORD, I WILL BE JOYFUL IN GOD MY SAVIOUR.**"

We must believe that God is our only hope – both in good times and bad. If we're only fair weather friends we're worse than unbelievers. How can we ever know the quality of our faith if it is never put to the test? What would be the point of having a prize racehorse in the stable if we never took it out for a gallop? The more training and exercise we give it, the stronger it will become and probably the more races it will win. So it is with us, as James 1v12 puts it: "Blessed is the man who perseveres under trial, because when he has stood the test, he will receive the crown of life that God has promised to those who love him."

Jesus, in the gospels, made it very clear what he thought of those that buried their talent in the ground and made no effort to be resourceful and enterprising. Don't get me wrong. I'm not advocating bootstrap, in-your- own- strength religion. No, no, a thousand times no. The whole thrust of Jesus' teaching is that those who have received the gift of God's Holy Spirit into their hearts need to be busy working it up and out until it turns into a veritable fountain of life refreshing all and sundry. And as we all know, that is easier said than done with the devil working overtime to thwart and frustrate our best endeavours.

How does our friend Job cope in the circumstances? God has lifted his hedge of protection and allowed Satan free rein to run riot and play merry hell with his life. He's lost all his children that he was praying for so steadfastly, now his health has broken down, and, as if that wasn't the last straw, his wife suggests it might be a good idea if he cursed God and dropped dead! This is surely too much for even a man of Job's renowned patience!

A reputation like that does not appear overnight like manna from heaven. It takes years of painstaking diligence and application. We saw at the outset that early in the morning he made sacrifices on behalf of his children when they'd been partying. He had developed over the years a right-living routine that was God-centred. He was fully committed to the extent that, as far as he was concerned, there was literally no other option available. There was no Plan B. These are the kind of folk that warm the cockles of God's heart, because God himself is just like that. He is fully committed to His plan of salvation for mankind – and there is no Plan B. There is no other way to come to Him except through Jesus Christ – crucified, resurrected, ascended into heaven, and soon to return to reign on earth, when every knee shall bow and every tongue confess that Jesus Christ is Lord, to the glory of God the Father.

Many find such a Christian claim offensively arrogant. What about all the other world religions? Are they of no account? Can there not be several paths up the same mountain all leading to the top? Humanly speaking, I have to admit that sounds eminently plausible. But the Spirit of God within convicts and convinces me otherwise, not to mention the very words of Jesus as recorded in the gospel of John: "I am the Way, the Truth and the Life. No man comes to the Father but by Me," which doesn't seem to allow much scope for liberal interpretation. No other major religion contains such a categorically unequivocal statement. If nothing else, the various "I ams" of Jesus should stop us in our tracks and make us realise he was someone quite extraordinary. "I am the light of the world", "I am the good shepherd", "I am the bread of life", "Before Abraham was I am", "I am the Messiah" (spoken to the woman at the well). These are extravagant claims which cannot be dismissed lightly as the ravings of a lunatic. They were all supported by well-observed and historically recorded signs and wonders.

Josephus, a respected Jewish historian living and writing in the first century A.D. had this to say in Book XVIII, chapter 3 of his famous Antiquities of the Jews: "Now, there was about this time, Jesus, a wise man, if it be lawful to call him a man, for he was a doer of wonderful works, - a teacher of such men as receive the truth with pleasure. He drew over to him both many of the Jews, and many of the gentiles. He was Christ; and when Pilate, at the suggestion of the principal men amongst us had condemned him to the cross, those that loved him at the first did not forsake him, for he appeared to them alive again the third day, as the divine prophets had foretold these and ten thousand other wonderful things concerning him; and the tribe of Christians, so named from him, are not extinct at this day." It's not just the gospels in the New Testament that bear witness to His historical reality.

On the evidence it is entirely reasonable for any sane thinking person to believe that Jesus is precisely who He claims to be – Almighty God's appointed and anointed Saviour of the world. In fact, the Bible tells us there is salvation in no other name.

However it is up to each individual to accept or reject God's provision for our redemption as he or she wishes. We have all been graciously endowed with free-will. How could it be otherwise? God is love, and love of its very nature cannot and will not be coerced. Perfect love has to allow the possibility of rejection. The tragedy is that the world, the flesh and the devil have deluded many into believing a lie and denying the freedom and fulfilment that comes from committing ourselves to the Way, the Truth and the Life found only in following Jesus.

Chapter 5

The Coming of the Comforters
(Job 2v11 – 5v27)

The devil had attacked Job. Now he was suffering
something awful in the flesh. Surely there could not be
any further affliction on the way? Don't you believe it!
When you're really reeling on the ropes, that's when the
world loves to put the boot in – and who better than Job's
three "friends"! Right on cue along come Eliphaz, Bildad
and Zophar. You will recall in chapter one these three
gentlemen were described as types of unsaved worldly
wise men – people who so often give the impression of
knowing all there is to know about God without actually
knowing Him at all. To them the concept of a saviour is
sheer nonsense because they believe that mankind is able
to save himself by dint of his own wit and will. Belief in
their own brilliance and know-how has blinded them.

Anyway, bad news travels fast and sure enough news of
Job's troubles soon reached these three. To their credit,

the bible tells us, they agreed to go at once and sympathise with him and comfort him. When they spied him from a distance they could hardly believe their eyes, he looked so terrible and utterly wretched. This puts me in mind of that old Stanley Holloway monologue "My word, you do look queer!", where all his friends gather round telling him how awful he looks until he is almost convinced he's about to pop his clogs. Then young Jenkins drops by and full of fun and enthusiasm says, "My word, you do look well! You're looking fine and in the pink." This perks him up no end, and leaping out of bed he replies, "You're right, old son. Come and have a drink. My word, I do feel well!" I think many of us when we visit the sick or try to sympathise with another's misfortune have forgotten the true meaning of "comfort". It comes from a latin word signifying "building up", "strengthening" and "encouraging". How successful Job's three friends were at doing this we shall soon see.

The sight of Job so shocked them they burst into tears, tore their robes and sprinkled dust on their heads. In those days this was the kind of thing you did when someone had died. Having already been told to drop dead by his wife, now his three chums come along and behave as if they were attending his funeral. What a great comfort they were! They then proceeded to sit around for a week without saying a word. Perhaps waiting to see if indeed he was going to snuff it. No point in wasting their precious words of wisdom on a dead dog. Alternatively this could be the one truly wise thing they all did throughout this sorry saga. I have so often found when with those in distress that their greatest need is not so much for words of comfort but simply for a shoulder to cry on. Just to be there is all that is necessary.

Having watched and waited in silence for seven long days the friends may well have been wondering what good they were doing and whether they ought not to be packing their bags, mounting their camels and heading for home. Plainly there didn't seem to be much they could do to help. They weren't medical men, and if Job wanted them to stay and chat he'd better say so. In the etiquette of the time it was up to Job, the greatest man in all the East, the host and local chieftain, to start any conversation. Only when he had had his say would the others be entitled to contribute their fourpenny worth.

At last Job rouses himself and starts speaking, thus commencing one of the most fascinating philosophical and theological discussions ever recorded – and to think that this all took place 3,500 years ago! Well, what did Job say for openers? You'd think he might have greeted his friends and thanked them for hanging around for so long sharing in his misery. Not a bit of it. No polite "How d'ye dos?" He dives straight in at the deep end. He curses the day he was born. Understandably, he is feeling rather more than somewhat sorry for himself, which is not unusual with those who are seriously ill.

What helps sustain the human spirit in such circumstances is the expectation, born of life's experience, that all sickness comes to pass. Whenever in the past I have been unwell, sooner or later I have recovered. When winter is upon us, we can always look forward to spring. Hope is the rope we all need to hang onto. Once we let go, despair sets in and we plunge into the devil's domain. Supposedly above the portals of Hades is inscribed the legend – 'Abandon hope all ye who enter herein'.

Apart from wishing he'd never been born, Job ponders what the point of life really is. What's the point of life for those who are miserable all the time? What's the point of life for those who drift and meander through it to no purpose? What's the point of life for those who do not have God to guide them? What's the point of a life that's constantly in turmoil? Then Job lets us into a little secret. "What I feared has come upon me. What I dreaded has happened to me." This is the man whom God said there was no one on earth like him, he was blameless and upright, he feared God and shunned evil.

There seems to be a slight incongruity here. There's an old hymn with the line: "Fear Him, ye saints, and you will then have nothing else to fear." The fear of the Lord is the beginning of wisdom, and Job certainly feared and revered God. So when he says, "What I feared has come upon me," what does he mean? Was he really not trusting

God after all, but just trusting to luck – and, hey presto, his luck had finally run out? Had he merely been going through a mumbo-jumbo series of religious rituals to keep God sweet and in his corner? I don't think so. For one, God would certainly not have thought so highly of him had this been the case. What then is the case?

We're going to have to wait a bit for the answer. The Bible is so often like this. It whets our appetite, but rarely gives us instant gratification. It is not for casual observers or superficial sightseers. We need to hang in there and press on into the deeper things of God. It takes time to be holy. Patience and longsuffering are characteristics of the Holy Spirit, as Job was in the process of finding out.

Now that Job has at last opened the batting, as it were, and posed the question, friend Eliphaz comes on to bowl an over or two believing that he has the answer to the problem. He starts a trifle diffidently not wishing at this stage to unduly upset the sick man.

"Please don't be short with me if I may be so bold as to venture a few of my own thoughts on the subject. I appreciate you are not quite your usual robust self and are in a considerably weakened condition. But just think back to when you were strong and healthy how you led the pack and set the pace. All of a sudden you're laid low and you're throwing in the towel. You've lived a decent, honest life, taking care of the less fortunate. You're famous for your good deeds. Surely all this should give you confidence and hope for the future?"

On the face of it this all seems like reasonably encouraging stuff. But there lies the subtlety of it. Our confidence is not to rest in our good deeds but in Christ Jesus who died for us and rose again.

Undeterred, Eliphaz earnestly persists with his argument. "How can the innocent ever be judged guilty? A loving heavenly Father can surely not destroy the upright?"

The trouble with this train of thought is that the Bible tells us "all have sinned and fallen short of the glory of God". However good we may appear to one another, in comparison with God we are very poor specimens indeed. What Eliphaz and the world find so hard to accept is that in God's sight we are all guilty as hell. So the only way we will ever make it is to shed our filthy rags and put on Jesus' robe of righteousness. How do we do that? Purely and simply by faith, believing that He is our Saviour and relying on His innocence and uprightness to save us from the wrath to come.

But dear old Eliphaz is only just getting started. "As I have observed, those who plough evil and those who sow trouble reap it," he continues, "so if you now find yourself in trouble, you've only got yourself to blame."

What a comforter he's turning out to be! The fallacy of this statement is that it completely ignores the possibility of mercy and forgiveness, and the grace and compassion of God. I don't deny that frequently we do reap what we sow, but it ain't necessarily so. Very often we may reap what others have planted, or others reap the rewards of our efforts. I only have to think of my children, who are the beneficiaries of the good things I have been able to pass on to them and also sadly the victims of the countless times I got it all horribly wrong.

"Look here, my friend, it is impossible to be more righteous than God. Let's face it, if He can chuck a third of the angels out of heaven because even they sinned, sure as hell what chance have we mere mortals got of getting away with anything scot-free. You'll just have to face the music and take your medicine with the rest, and accept that man is born to trouble as surely as sparks fly upward." All that Eliphaz is saying sounds perfectly logical but it is also saviourless and merciless. Not something designed to lift the spirit, or strengthen and encourage.

"If I were you," he carries on, "I'd appeal to God. If you have a complaint take it right to the top. He can work miracles, He has the weather at His beck and call. He blesses the humble and those that mourn, but stands against the proud and crafty. He supports the poor and needy and heals the brokenhearted. He'll protect you from disaster and keep your children safe and see you reach the end of your days healthy, wealthy and wise." I think Eliphaz got a little carried away here and forgot whom he was talking to. Job is presently sitting in an ashpit, sick as a parrot, having lost all his children and property.

What is Job to make of this diatribe? If and he isn't experiencing all the blessings of God in his life right now, then the only conclusion he can possibly draw is that he is the most miserable and undeserving of sinners. But he knows he's not; and God agrees.

Chapter 6

Job and Bildad

(Job 6v1 – 9v35)

After listening to the uncomforting words of Eliphaz, Job redoubles his efforts to convince his 'friends' that, all things considered, it would be a kindness for the Lord to let him die.

"I have not forsaken God, even though He seems to have forsaken me. Now you three roll up and turn out to be no help whatsoever. You see what a dreadful state I'm in and you're all scared stiff thinking, 'O my God, surely that couldn't happen to us, or could it?' I ask you to tell me where I've been wrong, and all you've given me thus far are theories that prove nothing. Please try and put yourself in my position for a moment. My very faith in God is hanging in the balance. Am I really as wicked as you imply. Have I somehow lost the ability to discern between good and evil? Am I unable to tell the difference between right or wrong?"

These days we can all too easily find ourselves living for so long in the greyness of spin and half-truths that almost without noticing we start thinking this is normal and right and proper. Our eyes become accustomed to the gloom. We are ceasing to walk in the light of God's word. Psalm 119v105 tells us, "His word is a lamp to our feet and a light for our path." So Job is asking, "Tell me, have I lost the plot with God? Are there words of His that I have completely misconstrued?" This is why it is so vital for all Christians to be constantly reading and studying the Bible. As soon as we stop, it is surprising how quickly we forget, and begin making up our own rules to suit the circumstances. We give ourselves the excuse the Bible is too old-fashioned and really doesn't address many of the problems we encounter today. We need 'new age' solutions for our 'new age' life-style. Right? Wrong! Some things never change, and God's word is as up-to-date today as it ever was, and we monkey around with it at our peril.

Job again turns his attention to his sorry plight. "Life is hardly worth living. Let's face it, the days are long and toilsome; at night I toss and turn racked with pain. Roll on the grave when all will at last be stillness and tranquility! God, why do you bother to get involved with us poor mortals? You're forever looking over our shoulders and setting us impossible tests. I wish you'd just leave me alone for a while. If I sin, what's that to you? What possible difference can it make in the overall scheme of things? But if I have sinned and it bugs you, why don't you simply pardon me? Soon enough I'll be dead and resting in peace unable to cause you any further trouble."

What fascinates me about dear old Job is how timelessly and honestly human he is. Three and a half millennia ago he was struggling with these notions. They are precisely the same questions many believers continue to wrestle with down to this very day. Interestingly, although Eliphaz was a fully paid up member of the tit-for-tat brigade – eye for eye and tooth for tooth, Job on the other hand knows that God is in the forgiveness business. His problem is that he doesn't know for what he needs to be forgiven. Also, he appears to believe that the grave is the end of all things as far as he is concerned. Nonetheless, later on in these discourses he is able to proclaim, "I know that my Redeemer lives, and that in the end He will stand upon the earth, and after my skin has been destroyed, yet in my flesh I will see God." But we mustn't get ahead of ourselves. We will have to wait to find out how he arrives at this conclusion.

Now Bildad, the Shuhite decides it's his turn to get a word in.

"How can you suggest such things?" Bildad protests archly. "God cannot ignore sin. He is the God of justice. He's not going to turn a blind eye to what your children have been getting up to. They quite properly got what was coming to them. But if you are as pure and upright as you claim, by all means plead with Him for yourself and I'm sure He will do what is right, and bless and prosper you beyond your wildest dreams." Friend Bildad is not exactly overflowing with the milk of human kindness and compassion!

His concept of God is a bit heartless to say the least. But, we need to bear in mind that he was around at a time when the "flood" was not yet ancient history. The world's population, except for Noah and his family, had been wiped out at a stroke by an "act of God" purportedly because of their violence and corruption. As mentioned in chapter 2 it is quite possible that folk who had actually spoken to Noah were still living in Job's day. This is why Bildad now suggests that some of the older generation might usefully be consulted to confirm what happens to people who become uncoupled from God and try to play fast and loose.

"Ask your elder relatives what they know about such things. Let's face it, we're mere saplings in the forest of history. Surely God does not reject a blameless man, nor tolerate evildoers. That being the case, have no fear, my friend, you'll soon be up and about again laughing and joking as if nothing had happened." The trouble with these words of cold comfort was that they simply did not address the facts of the matter. Laughing and joking would have been the last things on Job's mind right now.

You can almost hear him screaming at Bildad in sheer frustration, "I am as blameless as I know how to be, and yet I am still suffering. Plainly your understanding of God is not quite as simplistic as you are trying to make out." Job now contemplates the enormity of God and realises the vastness of the chasm that separates and differentiates Him from fallible mortals. "He alone stretches out the heavens and treads on the waves of the sea." This at once brings to mind Jesus walking on the water. "He performs wonders that cannot be fathomed, miracles that cannot be numbered. He can do anything He pleases and no one can stop Him. How could anyone argue the toss with such a One. However innocent I believed myself to be, however just my cause, in God's sight all I could do would be to plead for mercy."

Job was well aware of, and had a healthy respect for, the almightiness of God. This is where hi-tec, scientific modern man has completely lost it. We're altogether too sophisticated to believe there is a purposeful, creative intelligence so far above and beyond our own that it can only be comprehended through the medium of faithful, humble prayer, worship and total submission. As soon as we jump on our high horse thinking we can manage our affairs quite nicely, thank you, that's exactly when we start running into the buffers or over the precipice. Today's secular humanistic democracies are proof enough that mankind left to its own resources is incapable of coming up with the right answers to save this planet in the long term; not to mention the ever increasing poverty, sickness, greed, violence and general lawlessness that is evident everywhere.

As Job's musings on the nature of God continue it is becoming apparent that he is unaware that Satan is the real culprit. Admittedly Satan can do no more than God permits, but it is he who tempts and tests and tries our faith hoping to trip us up and make us fall. Thankfully Psalm 37vv23-24 tells us, "The Lord delights in the way of the man whose steps he has made firm; though he stumble he will not fall, for the Lord upholds him with His hand."

"I am blameless," Job insists, "so it's clear to me that God treats the good and the bad just the same. How have I benefited from being a law-abiding, God-fearing, upstanding citizen? When a wicked dictator comes to power and perverts the course of justice, if God is not there allowing it to happen, then who is? The trouble is, God, you are too great and I am too insignificantly small to be able to figure any of this out. The gap twixt thee and me is altogether too wide for us to meet together and talk these things through on a man to man basis. If only there were someone to arbitrate between us, to lay his hand upon us both, someone to remove your rod from me, so that I need no longer be terrified of you. Then I would speak up fearlessly, but as it now stands, how can I possibly?"

Job in his mental meanderings has suddenly hit upon God's plan of salvation for mankind. Only someone who is both human and divine at one and the same time could do the trick. Job knows of no such person. 3,500 years on we can see that Jesus Christ was and is the very one that he had in mind those millennia ago who completely fills the bill. No other religion in the world provides such a perfect solution to the problem of mankind's incompatability and irreconcilability with God.

Chapter 7

Zophar – so good!

(Job 10v1 – 14v22)

In Job's present state of health, if the admonition, "Love your neighbour as yourself," were applied by him, he would be a most unpleasant grouch to all around. His self-pity party was fast turning itself into an almost suicidal self-loathing. "Why me, God? Tell me what it is I'm supposed to have done wrong to warrant all this aggravation. Why did you bother to go to the trouble of giving me life, and letting me taste the good times, only to tear me apart and destroy me like this? As things now stand I am hopelessly confused, and have no idea what I need to do to please you. I beg of you, just leave me be and let me die in peace. Your awesome power and perfection are altogether too much for me."

When we find ourselves wallowing around like warthogs in the slough of despond it's important to remember 1 Corinthians 10v13: "And God is faithful; He will not let you be tested beyond what you can bear. But when you are tested, He will also provide a way out so that you can stand up under it." If any of Job's comforters had come up with that verse of scripture at this juncture I don't reckon for a minute that he would have particularly thanked them for it. But we all need to keep verses like this well bedded down in our hearts, so that, when storms occur, our faith is bolstered by them.

Now we meet Job's third friend, Zophar, whom one assumes is younger than the others, having obligingly waited for his elders and betters to have their say first. He has clearly become exasperated with Job's insistence that, as far as he's concerned, he's done nothing wrong to deserve the calamities that have befallen him.

So, without any 'by-your-leaves' or 'excuse-mes', Zophar joins the fray and throws his hat into the ring.

"There you go jabbering on, talking the hind leg off a donkey while we meekly listen in silence. Someone needs to put you right. You're spouting nonsense. You insist you're blameless and your understanding of the Almighty is flawless. Well, let me tell you, you are most definitely not sinless in God's sight. What makes you think you can fathom the mysteries of God any better than anyone else? If He comes along and dishes out punishment it must be justified. God simply does not make mistakes. Of His very nature He knows exactly what He is doing."

Once again a saviourless, compassionless gospel is being

preached. Zophar suffers from the same misapprehension as his pals. He is a staunch believer in affliction coming as a result of wickedness on our part - the sowing and reaping principle. We already looked at this earlier and saw that it completely ignores the possibility of grace, mercy, and forgiveness; not to mention the inadequacy of any humanly devised form of sacrifice to compensate for our holiness deficiency, which blocks our way into the Holy of Holies. As we now know, Jesus is that full, perfect and sufficient sacrifice for our sins. At the end of the last chapter you will recall that Job was pleading with God for a go-between. Praise the Lord, He supplies all our needs according to His glorious riches in Christ Jesus *(Philippians 4v19).*

Another thing about 'sowing and reaping' is that it overlooks the fact, many wicked people do seem to get away with murder much of the time. We have the expression, "The devil looks after his own." Good times and bad times come to all. They are there to test the quality of our faith, and even bring us to faith in God. If we can always cope in our own strength and live very comfortably within our means there is not much call for faith in our lives. It's when the house burns down and the ship sinks that we need to reach out above and beyond ourselves towards God. That's when we discover that there truly is another dimension to life – the spiritual realm where the supernatural kicks in, and God's will is done on earth as it is in heaven. If it were not so, why would Jesus have taught us the Lord's Prayer?

Zophar continues, "If only you really loved God and cleaned up your act, I can assure you that in no time at all these troubles of yours would be over and done with. You'd be living safe and secure as ever with no one to be afraid of." I'm sure that's just what Job wanted to hear, I don't think! How patronizingly condescending!

Indeed, Job answers Zophar and the rest of them in kind, "Doubtless you are the only wise ones left on earth. How will we manage when you pass on? Don't you think I know a thing or two as well? I wasn't born yesterday! What you say in theory sounds plausible enough, but from where I'm sitting right now it's a fat lot of help! It's all very well for you guys to philosophise over my misfortune when you're all right, Jack! You'd better watch out, because there but for the grace of God you go too. I know in my heart that I'm innocent and whatever you say will not persuade me otherwise. Anyway, how do you account for all the godless rogues out there seemingly enjoying trouble-free lives? God can do whatever He wishes. I only wish He wouldn't pick on me! There's something going on here I really don't understand. If only I could speak to the Almighty and discuss my case with Him. As for you three, what a worthless bunch of doctors you've turned out to be! The kindest and wisest thing you could have done would be to keep your mouths shut. If God took a shine to test you like He's testing me, how do you think you would fare? I bet you'd be in the same boat, and then where would all your fine phrases about justice and sowing and reaping be?"

We need to remember what Jesus said in Matthew 5v45: "God causes His sun to rise on the evil and the good, and sends rain on the righteous and the unrighteous." Or as some wag paraphrased it:

> The rain it raineth every day
>
> Upon the just and unjust fella;
>
> But more upon the just,
>
> 'Cos the unjust's got the just's umbrella!

It's not the circumstances but our reaction to them that is crucial. Do we treat them as stepping-stones or stumbling blocks? Are they opportunities or obstacles? Job was slowly learning that life is not always fair. But he was aware that ultimately all things come from God and so He is quite entitled to take them back again any time, just as he admitted at the outset when his children and property were all destroyed, "The Lord gave and the Lord has taken away. Blessed be the name of the Lord!"

As Job's friends waffle on, I sense his mounting frustration. Talking about God is getting him nowhere. He realises that talking to God is the only way to go. How true this is of Christians today. We can sit in holy huddles talking about God until the cows come home. It's only when we get on our knees in fervent prayer that any real progress is made. So now Job speaks directly to the Lord.

"God, for starters, heal this dreadful sickness and stop terrifying me." There's no messing about with Job. He comes straight to the point. He's long past the stage of, "If it be thy will," or "Please and I would be ever so grateful." He's at the end of his tether. He's confused and angry and miserable. He's reaching out to God like a little child yelling desperately for comfort and reassurance from its mother. "Now God, we need to talk. Why are you letting me suffer all this aggro? Fair's fair, I can accept a bit of trouble now and then, but this is just too much to bear. I know that life is not a bowl of cherries, but neither is it supposed to be only the stones. If this is the hand you're determined to deal me, then count me out! I'd be better off in the grave, waiting for your trumpet call when you will, I know, eventually cover over all my sin and reinstate me in your good grace once more."

Isn't that prayer of Job's interesting? He believed in atonement for sin and the resurrection of the righteous. His friends were a bit flakey on these fundamental Judeo-Christian principles, but this has to be what gave Job his abiding faith and hope. Come what may, he knew that his redeemer lived and would be standing on the earth at the latter day.

Chapter 8

I know That My Redeemer Lives

(Job 15v1 – 19v29)

Not only is Job frustrated, but so are his companions. They are ladling out all sorts of loveless theological medicine and Job won't swallow it.

"Look here," says Eliphaz, "There's absolutely no doubt you're a sinner. Why, you're being well nigh blasphemous, accusing God of injustice! What makes you think you know so much more about Him than we do?" He now repeats his original argument, "If God can toss a third of the angels out of heaven because, even in that holy place, they were able to sin and rebel, fat chance we, mere men of the world, have of being found blameless in His eyes?" On the face of it, that's not a bad point, and essentially he is right. We are indeed all born with a sinful nature whether we like it or not.

Eliphaz warms to his subject, "Listen to me and I will explain a thing or two that I've had handed down to me from the wise men of old, when no foreigners walked the land." Sounds like this is harking back to Noah and his immediate family, before they went forth and multiplied. "Wicked, godless men live in constant torment and terror. They have no one to turn to in time of trouble. They may shake their fists at God and boast that they can get along perfectly happily without Him, but they know in their heart of hearts a day of reckoning is coming. All they have worked for and trusted in will prove to be worthless. All their plotting and scheming will come to nothing."

This could easily have been passed down from the mouth of Noah. He had had first hand experience of the wrath of God when the flood came and washed away all the wicked. What Eliphaz says here is basically true, except that it seems to deny the possibility of God's grace. Remember, Noah found grace in the eyes of the Lord, and down through the ages God's grace has been available to all who truly seek Him. Even so, I'm not sure that what Eliphaz had to say was much consolation, or indeed relevant, to poor old Job's case.

Nevertheless, our hero once more wearily rouses himself in reply.

"What depressing comforters you've turned out to be! If you were in my place I too could trot out a few fancy arguments and wag my finger at you. But that's not my style. I'd try to encourage and comfort and bring you relief. All you've succeeded in doing is wear me out. I am devastated. I've lost everything I ever held dear. God has deserted me and now I'm mocked and jeered at by all and sundry. What harm have I done to anyone? My conscience is clear. I will continue to make my prayers and supplications with a pure heart. I know there must be someone in heaven who will take my part and intercede for me as a friend. Lord, you are the only one I can look to. You are the only Way I know, despite the trials and tribulations I am presently going through."

Job's conviction that we surely have an advocate interceding for us at God's right hand is New Testament theology staring out at us from the oldest book in the Bible. As is always said, 'What in the Old Testament was concealed, in the New is revealed.' This was the difference between Job and his mates. They were basically formulaic religionists. They certainly believed in the existence of God. How could they not? – what with Noah only about ten generations removed. But that was also their problem. The memory of what God did in Noah's day convinced them that He was all to do with catastrophic floods, justice and judgment. As a result many reckoned that discretion was the better part of valour, and it was best to leave God well alone. He wasn't the kind of person you wanted to tangle with. Just stay away from the kind of things that might upset Him and try and live a quiet and peaceable life, but otherwise steer clear of any close involvement. How many so-called

Christians do you know like that?

A bloodless, relationless religion soon gives rise to litanies, liturgies and other formulae for maintaining one's good standing. Don't get me wrong. There's nothing the matter with disciplined routine, provided it doesn't turn itself into religion by numbers, six 'Our Fathers', ten 'Hail Marys', once a week in church and 50p in the offertory. All the while God, for His part, is just yearning for a meaningful one to one relationship where the involvement is so intimately entwined that He is literally in us and we are in Him. It is easy enough to see where these early theological thinkers were coming from. But what started as a trickle is now a fast flowing river with many tributaries representing the saviourless, graceless, unforgiving and sometimes heartless faiths the world is flooded with today.

Job is not done yet, "Come, come now, you smart Alecs, I don't believe there's a wise one amongst you! You guys call black, white. When it's pitch dark, you say it's light. According to you there's no hope for me – and if that's the case, then I guess there's no hope for you either. We can all go together when we go. What a wretched prospect!"

Now Bildad pops up again. As if his last contribution hadn't been enough! He had suggested that Job's kids had only got what was coming to them and that if Job himself was prepared to smarten up his act he'd be back in God's good graces in no time at all. So what's he got to say this time around?

"Stop calling us stupid and be sensible a moment. You're ranting and raving like a child throwing a tantrum. You're not the only pebble on the beach. Let me assure you that the wicked do indeed get their come-uppance. They may fool themselves into thinking they are all safe and secure, but in the twinkling of an eye their world comes crashing down about their ears. Mark my words, that's the way it is for the godless of this world."

Once again Bildad's interjection is less than helpful. Job's world has come crashing down about his ears, so the only inference he can draw from what has just been said is that he too is godless. But that is clearly not so.

Where does Job go from here? "Thanks for nothing!" he says, "You seem to take delight in telling me it's all my fault and I'm only getting my just deserts. If that were true I'd be obliged if you kept your nose out of my business. Instead, you act all smug and self-righteous, which only adds to my humiliation. I am telling you for the umpteenth time that I've been wronged. I cry out to the Lord but get no response.

"My friends and relatives have all abandoned me. I've lost the respect of my employees and I've become the butt of everyone's jokes. I am only just surviving by the skin of my teeth. Is it too much to ask of you, my only friends left, to have pity on me? What you've said to me thus far has frankly not been a great comfort. Surely you can't enjoy making sport of me like the rest?

"Nevertheless, irrespective of what you lot think, **I KNOW THAT MY REDEEMER LIVES** and that in the end He will stand triumphantly upon the earth. Even though, right now, it feels that He is determined to kill me, I know that He will raise me up and I will see God. Yes, yes, yes! I myself will see Him in the flesh! But if you are so set on judging me, you need to beware of the judgment to come that will be meted out on you."

Wow! That is some statement of faith on Job's part. This is the kind of declaration that can only be made by divine revelation. It's on a par with Peter's confession when Jesus asked him, "Who do you say I am?" and Peter replied, "You are the Christ of God – the Messiah!"

Have you noticed that throughout these discourses, and even before, Job is constantly addressing himself to God, yet never once have his friends done so? They are great in their own eyes at talking about God, but their personal relationship with Him seems to be non-existent. This puts me in mind of religious discussion programmes on the radio so often chaired by self-confessed unbelievers and even atheists. Job, on the other hand, displays all the characteristics of a genuinely deep and heartfelt attachment. His faith is being sorely tried, but he is hanging in there regardless.

Chapter 9

The Discomforters!

(Job 20v1 – 24v25)

When we last heard from Zophar he was preaching a saviourless, compassionless gospel. I wonder if he has changed his tune. Is it possible that Job's astonishing revelation about a living redeemer has in any way affected him? Has this leopard changed his spots?

"What you have been saying puzzles me. In fact, you have been rather insulting," says Zophar somewhat peevishly. "Surely you must know how it goes with the wicked in this world. They may enjoy the pleasures of sin for a season, but when you look again they have vanished without trace. It was ever thus. There is no rest for the wicked. The more they crave, the more they want. Yet their treasure will never save or satisfy them, nor will it last. In the midst of plenty, disaster will strike. God will see to it that they come to a miserable end."

What a jolly companion he has turned out to be! The

consensus wisdom in Zophar's day was that bad things only happened to bad people. He and his chums were obviously doing very nicely, thank you, which would indicate that they were in God's good books. This entitled them, in their view, to look disapprovingly down their long noses on lesser mortals who were having a tough time of it. Such a mindset became so ingrained into the middle-eastern culture that we find it still very much in evidence in the New Testament.

At one point, Jesus says to his disciples, "I tell you the truth, it is hard for a rich man to enter the Kingdom of Heaven. Again I tell you, it is easier for a camel to go through the eye of a needle than for a rich man to enter the Kingdom of God." This so astounded his followers that they said, "Who then can be saved?" The thinking was that anyone who was wealthy was manifestly under the blessing of God. So naturally when the saints go marching in the rich will be at the front of the parade. "Not so," says Jesus. Being saved has nothing whatever to do with our material wealth or lack of it. It has everything to do with calling upon the name of the Lord and committing oneself wholeheartedly into His hands. The prosperity gospel, popular with so many televangelists, is a close relative of this doctrine. So beware!

What is Job to make of all this? His 'comforters' are still singing from the same song sheet. "O.K. fellows, mock on if you must, but do me this one favour; just hear me out," he pleads as he continues. "I'm not blaming you for my catastrophic state of affairs, so I can see no reason for you to be taking umbrage and feeling insulted. All things considered, if I'm a bit short with you that's fairly understandable in my present circumstances.

"Terror and confusion grips me the more I ponder my lot. How is it that the wicked are living untroubled and even successful lives, while here I am sitting in the ashpit? They are partying and having a high old time, giving not a second thought to God and saying, 'Who is the Almighty, that we should pay Him any mind? What on earth is the point of praying to Him?' Despite all this, they could never persuade me to join them. One way or another I know they are travelling on the broadway to destruction.

"Who are we, to be trying to second guess God? Is there anything God doesn't know that we can teach Him? Of course not! Sooner or later we all have to die, rich and poor alike, noble and ignoble side by side in the grave. The Lord is no respecter of persons – He is Lord of all.

"But I bet I know what you guys are thinking. You're saying to yourselves, 'Alright, big shot, where's your house and family now? What right have you got to get on your high horse and pontificate to us?' Well, let me tell you a thing or two about the real world. Have you never noticed the fancy funerals that evil men have and the monuments that are erected in their honour? So how can you possibly console me with all this nonsense of yours about only the good and the godly living out their lives in peace and plenty. It's patently not true."

It is slowly dawning on Job that his troubles are not necessarily God-inflicted. Although he is well aware of the angels rebelling and being evicted from heaven, any knowledge of Satan's role in the spirit realm seems to have eluded him. Of course, the devil can only do what God permits, but Job and his pals were apparently oblivious to this aspect of him as accuser, tempter and general harasser, especially of believers. This is what was getting Job so hopelessly confused. He truly loved, feared and worshipped God and was convinced that the Lord was his refuge and protector and only had his best interests at heart. So how come all this tragedy had suddenly been dumped on him? I really sympathise with his predicament. In his position I would also be turning to God and crying out, "For heaven's sake, what is going on here?"

Something we all need to bear in mind is that Satan's main purpose is to give believers a hard time. This was, after all, the root cause of Job's troubles. In which case, we need to be worried if we are finding our lives pleasantly trouble-free! The truly committed Christian is going to find him or herself in the thick of it as often as not. The world does not march to the beat of God's drum. In fact it is marching down a different highway altogether. Jesus and the apostles all had it tough, because true Christianity is challenging and confrontational. The love it talks about is self-sacrificial. It is life-changing stuff. The world, the flesh and the devil don't like it, and will do their damnedest to stop it.

At this point, Eliphaz thinks he'll give it one more shot to try and convince Job that he is a miserable sinner, and all he needs is to repent of his evil ways to make everything in the garden come up roses again.

"My friend, you over-estimate your importance to God. What difference do you think it makes to Him if you are righteous? It cannot possibly add anything to the sum total of His righteousness. Therefore, it must be your lack of righteousness that is the root of the problem." An interesting premise to justify a specious argument! It also gives Eliphaz the opportunity to vent a whole load of spleen on his supposed friend, which suggests they were not such great mates after all.

"You really are a wicked old rogue! You loan-sharked your brothers, you short-changed your business associates, and demanded money with menaces. You lorded it over your tenants, charging them extortionate rent, leaving them starving and penniless. You showed no compassion to the poor and hungry. Is it any wonder you now find yourself in such a mess?

"Don't you think God sees what's going on? Although

He's above the highest heavens, you'd better believe there's nothing that escapes His notice. In olden times the wicked thought God was letting them get away with it. They said, "What can the Almighty do to us anyway?' It was then that the flood came and swept them all away. Job, old boy, you'd better repent, and quick. Then you will be restored to your former glory. Your prayers will be answered and success and prosperity will break out like never before."

With friends like Eliphaz who needs enemies? They are all treating the old man like a punch-bag. While he's down and almost out they seem to take great pleasure in putting the boot in. According to God, Job is blameless and so he could not possibly be guilty of all the dastardly crimes Eliphaz accuses him of. Once again the advice given is no help whatsoever. Job realises if he wants answers the only place to go is to God Himself. But that's easier said than done when He is apparently not listening to his prayers.

"If only I knew where to find Him," Job sighs. "I'm sure I'm sufficiently innocent and upright to come before the Lord and plead my case. But where is He when I need Him so badly? No way can He not know where I am at and what I am going through. When this is all over, tested as I am in the furnace of affliction, I guess I'll be a better man for it. But right now, I just wish it weren't so excruciatingly painful.

"Of course God can do whatever He pleases. That's one of the privileges of being God! Even so, I'm scared to think what else He may have in store for me. But this fear prompts me to want to talk with Him all the more to better understand His plans and purposes."

Job then comes up with a curious notion. "On reflection, it would be enormously helpful if God kept an appointments diary and let us know on what day of the week, or month, or year He was to visit and go over the accounts with us. As it presently stands, everyone is playing fast and loose, raping, pillaging and looting as if there were no tomorrow, in the belief that they will never be called to account." The truth is, if we knew for sure the day of God's visitation, faith would no longer be required. What's more, even if it were so, the Bible tells us that many would continue to ignore the approaching fateful day, thinking they could avoid it if they wished when the time came, just like we cancel any old visit to the doctor or dentist if it's inconvenient and doesn't suit our schedule. We all need reminding regularly that there is a Day of Reckoning coming, regardless of whether we fancy the idea or not! Our eventual appointment with God is one that cannot be cancelled, however inconvenient it may turn out to be!

Chapter 10

My God, My God,
Why Have You Forsaken Me?

(Job 25v1 – 31v40)

Job has just about succeeded in silencing his critics. But Bildad insists on sticking his oar in once more.

"God is almighty, all-knowing and ever-present. He is a God of order and He is commander-in-chief of the numberless hosts of heaven. He sees everything that is going on. You've just admitted as much yourself. How then is it possible for a mere mortal to be righteous in God's eyes? From childhood up we are bound to get it wrong and sin sometime or another. Purity before God is an absolute impossibility for the likes of us. Job, you are crazy to think otherwise. Compared with God we are mere maggots. No way can we be sinless." Well, there's a real word of encouragement to help bring Job's temperature down!

Bildad's mistake all along has been to confuse

righteousness with sinlessness, which is what sowers and reapers tend to do. Paul in Romans 4 explains it very well. He discusses the futility of trying to observe the Mosaic law to the letter, and therefore the impossibility of leading a sinless life. No amount of good works will ever suffice to wipe out the stain of sin. He then looks at the life of pre-Mosaic Abraham. It was not by virtue of his good works and keeping of God's laws that made him righteous. It was because he believed God and had a vibrant, vital relationship with Him. That was what made him blameless and upright in God's sight. And that's what is able to make all of us righteous before God, especially as Jesus is now at God's right hand as our advocate and mediator interceding for us. He it is who has atoned for our sin, and as it were wiped the slate clean, so that we can now approach the Throne of Grace with a clear conscience, in full assurance of faith, as Hebrews 10v22 puts it.

Many folk are kept from salvation by the notion, "How can a sinner like me possibly be a Christian. I'd feel such a hypocrite." The good news is that, contrary to popular belief, Christianity is tailor-made for sinners! All we need is a heartfelt desire for a second chance. God is forgiving and merciful. Our sinfulness fades into insignificance in God's sight as we put on the robe of righteousness supplied in the person of Jesus. As we open up our hearts to allow His spirit to dwell in us and we develop a personal relationship with Him, we become righteous too. This does not mean we will never sin again. We will stumble from time to time, but provided we are looking to and relying on Him, He will always be there to pick us up, dust us off and get us back on the right road. So you see, it is perfectly possible to be a 'sinner' saved by grace and at the same time 'righteous'. Think of human friendships. They don't break up because of the odd let down. They build up over many years and there's an elasticity in the relationship that makes allowances for acknowledged weaknesses and foibles. I believe our relationship with God is just like that. He knows all our peculiarities and why we are prone to trip up now and then. All He asks is that we stay close, and slowly but surely we will find ourselves being transformed into the kind of person He really wants us to be.

Job was by this time probably fed up to the back teeth with Bildad and his cronies, so he now indulges in a spat of sarcasm. "What a great help you've proved to be! You've cheered me up no end! What fantastic insight and wisdom you have displayed! What amazing spirituality! Just ponder a moment. God created the heavens and all that is in the universe. He spread out the stars in the skies and suspended the earth in space. Who are we to imagine that our puny minds could ever understand the merest fraction of what He is up to and how He goes about His business? Yet you have the audacity to judge me as if you were God

Himself, and tell me that I am more of a sinner than you lot. No way, Jose! I will never admit you are right, to my dying day. I believe in God and I will cling to that belief come what may. He has to be my redeemer and the only hope I or, for that matter, any of us have.

"Compare this to the godless. What chance have they ultimately got? They have no one to run to when in trouble, no one to deliver them, no one to delight in, no one to call upon at any time of the day or night. Whatever they manage to achieve in life will be no more than wood, hay and stubble and burnt up as easily. Though they go to the highest heights and the deepest depths and discover all manner of treasures, they will never find wisdom and understanding however clever and techno-brilliant they may be.

"Where does wisdom come from, and where does understanding dwell? Only God knows where it can be found. In truth and in fact, the fear of the Lord – that is where it begins, and to avoid evil is to start understanding a thing or two."

This is where modern science has led us all astray. Secular humanity believes that the more scientific knowledge we acquire, the cleverer we become, and so eventually we will have the answers to everything imaginable. In such a scenario God becomes superfluous and eventually irrelevant. Poor deluded fools that we are. The greater our knowledge, the greater our need for

God's guidance on how best to use that knowledge. One only has to consider the moral maze we are in with the genome project, DNA and cloning. The mind boggles at where all this could be leading.

The truth is, the more we discover, the more we find there is to discover. By way of analogy, think of an uninflated balloon. The little bit of air inside represents what we know, and the external surface area is the sum total of what we know we don't know. As we puff more knowledge into our balloon the external surface area increases accordingly. So, although we know a lot more, we also know that there is a lot more out there to know – and so it will go on ad infinitum, presumably until it bursts! Then where will all that knowledge be? This is why, however many plans we may have, however many great ideas we may come up with, it is vital that God's wisdom be our guide. It is not worldly knowledge that will solve our problems, but only divine wisdom. For starters it would be wise for us to develop a healthy respect for the omniscience, omnipotence and omnipresence of our Lord and realise that we do not, and never can, possess such attributes.

Job continues his musings. He reminisces about the 'good old days' before disaster struck. He talks of his intimate friendship with God like being bathed in celestial light. He prospered in all he did. He felt he was living on cloud nine. He was a respected city elder and people hung on his every word. He was a friend to the poor and needy. Had he died at that point in time monuments and memorials would have been erected in his honour.

Without warning tragedy struck. Suddenly his life was turned upside-down. Those who formerly fawned on him now mock him. All respect has been stripped away. He is despised and rejected. As if all this mental anguish were not enough, he is also in considerable physical pain and no one seems to want to lift a finger to help. Friends and family have all deserted him. Now he cries out to the Lord, "My God, my God, why have you forsaken me?"

Doesn't this sound familiar? Jesus was despised and rejected. His disciples all ran away in His hour of need. Then, on the cross, He cries out, "My God, my God, why have you forsaken me?" Clearly God is trying to tell us something fundamental to the Christian life.

God is not just for Christmas when the presents are being handed out and everyone is merry and having a jolly time. He is in the business of building integrity of character into each of us who will entrust ourselves into His hands. Whether we are on top of the world or down in the dumps, either way, it should make no difference to the course we steer and our commitment to the Lord. Without integrity we disintegrate when the going gets tough. This is particularly evident nowadays whenever accidents occur. Stress and trauma counsellors are at the scene almost as quickly, and in as many numbers, as the emergency services. I suppose in some respects Job's comforters were endeavouring to fill that role. But as far as stress and trauma were concerned, Job was in a better condition to cope than most. His integrity and firm belief in the sovereignty of God would see him through.

It is ironic really – for nothing has changed in 3,500 years. Job's stress counsellors were about as helpful as many of their counterparts are today. Without the wisdom of God to guide, it is very much a matter of the blind leading the blind. Nevertheless, I am aware there are lots of fine Christian organisations in the field of social work that do wonderful things in times of crisis. After all, this is where true believers can really come into their own and show their mettle, as Daniel 11v32 tells us, "Those that know their God are strong and get the job done."

By way of illustration of Job's integrity we hear him say, "I have vowed never to look lustfully at a girl. If I ever allowed myself to be seduced by a woman or had thoughts of committing adultery, then let my wife sleep around with whomever she pleases. If I dreamt of doing such a shameful thing I'd rightly deserve all the retribution I got."

You don't get many of his sort to the pound these days! Modern civilization on its travels down the centuries has lost a few suitcases en route. Some would claim it was unnecessary baggage anyway. I somehow don't think so.

These ancient worthies knew a thing or two it would be well for us to recollect also. Job's motivation for keeping on the straight and narrow is simple enough. How could he face God if he acted in any other way? Plainly the most important thing in Job's life was his relationship with the Lord. Without it he would be lost – as indeed we all would be. Shame is that so few realise it.

"If I've acted unjustly, turned a blind eye to the poor, ignored the widows and orphans, failed to feed the hungry or give a drink to the thirsty, if I've not been hospitable to strangers, clothed the naked, tended the sick or visited the prisoner, what will I do when God confronts me? What can I say when called to account?" Job admits, "For fear of God's awesome splendour I could not neglect to do such things." Would that we in this day and age had such a healthy respectful fear of the Lord.

All the things Job lists here are amazingly similar to the end-times parable Jesus told in Matthew 25. "Then the King will say to those on His right, 'Come, you who are blessed of my Father; take your inheritance, the kingdom prepared for you since the creation of the world. For I was hungry and you gave me something to eat, I was thirsty and you gave me something to drink, I was a stranger and you invited me in, I needed clothes and you clothed me, I was sick and you looked after me, I was in prison and you came to visit me.'

"Then the righteous will answer Him, 'Lord, when did we see you hungry and feed you, or thirsty and give you something to drink? When did we see you a stranger and invite you in, or needing clothes and clothe you? When did we see you sick or in prison and go to visit you?'

"The King will reply, 'I tell you the truth, whatever you did for one of the least of these brothers of mine, you did for me.'"

What Jesus told us in this parable was nothing new. 1,500 years earlier Job was already living by the self-same doctrine! He then goes on to foreswear the love of money or any other form of idolatry. He flatly refuses to let anything come between him and his love of God.

He continues to rack his brain for other types of sin that could be separating him from his beloved Lord. Had he possibly rejoiced and gloated over his enemy's misfortune? Had he, in a moment of weakness, cursed someone? Had he concealed a sin, like many do, and failed to confess it because he was more scared of losing face with his chums, than of humbling himself before God. No, he couldn't see anything that would account for his present troubles. In desperation he appeals to God. "Oh that someone up there would listen to me! Let the Almighty answer me and tell me what's wrong. I'm utterly baffled. Why am I having to suffer so, when far less deserving cases are seemingly getting off scot-free?"

In chapter 5, you will recall, I deferred comment on

Job's remark, "What I feared has come upon me; what I dreaded has happened to me." At the time, I said that we were going to have to wait a bit for the answer to what this really meant. I have heard preachers explain it by saying that if we are sufficiently fearful of something happening we can almost bring it upon ourselves. The theory being that deep down Job was a materialist at heart and his wealth was the bedrock of his security and he was therefore terrified of losing it all. So, when D (for Disaster) Day predictably arrives it is no more than self-fulfilling prophecy. He had subconsciously convinced himself that it was bound to happen sooner or later anyway.

Without wishing to deny the validity of such a scenario with certain types of folk, quite frankly, I don't buy it in Job's case! It is altogether too out of character. To start with, when Job lost all his possessions he merely said, "Naked I came from my mother's womb, and naked I shall depart. The Lord gave and the Lord has taken away. Praise the Lord!" This doesn't sound to me like a man who is suffering great mental anguish over his financial loss. The western world's cultural mindset today is so strongly materialistic that we run the risk of assuming that people have always thought this way. Job's priorities were of a different order.

So, what was it that Job was afraid of? Job, whom God proclaimed to be blameless and righteous. Could he have possibly been suffering from some secret phobia? I doubt it. What really gave him the heebie-jeebies was the fear of losing touch with God. His relationship with the Lord was what sustained him at every turn. Now suddenly, for no apparent reason, God has gone AWOL!

When I was very young I remember going with my mother on the London Underground. I was only a toddler, and my mother always walked at a very purposeful pace, which meant I had to trot to keep up. I lagged behind as we hurried on down interminable dimly lit tunnels with crowds rushing in all directions. Suddenly I lost touch. My mother was nowhere to be seen. Panic gripped me and I burst into floods of tears. People stopped to comfort me, but I was inconsolable. "Mummy, mummy, where've you gone? I'm lost!" After what seemed like an age my mother reappeared and all was well once more.

This, I believe, is how Job felt – just like Jesus on the cross at Calvary - and this is how all of us should feel, when we lose touch with God. If we don't, then our relationship with Him is not quite what it ought to be, nor the way God wants it to be.

Semi-detached Christians are the bane of today's church. They are the one foot in, one foot out, hokey-cokey brigade! Seven whole days, not one in seven is the commitment we are called to. But it doesn't end there. With Him in us and we in Him, Jesus is using us as living stones to build His church. This means we are being fitted, committed and interconnected one to another, so that when a brother or sister in Christ hurts, we hurt too. When they rejoice, it makes us glad.

"In my Father's house are many mansions," Jesus famously told His disciples in John 14. This always puzzled me as a child. I understood a mansion to be a small palace. So, how could lots of palaces manage to fit inside a house? In fact, a better translation of what He said is, "In my Father's house there's plenty of room – there's no shortage of space; if it were not so I would have told you." The point I am leading up to is that there is only one house in which we all live together – no semi-detacheds or separate apartments. Involvement is the name of the game, dwelling together in unity, harmony and one anotherness.

We are all supposed to be under the one roof. As soon as we come out from under we put ourselves at risk by jettisoning all the support mechanisms available to us whilst we stay within the fold. It is then we cry out contrarily, "My God, why have you forsaken me," when in truth it is usually we who have turned our backs on Him.

We need to beware of taking liberties with the free will God has so graciously given to each of us. To my mind the saddest verse in the bible comes after Samson's fun and games with Delilah. When he awoke the next morning 'he knew not that the Lord was no longer with him'. He assumed the power of God would be forever at his beck and call. That's not the way it works. As the Lord's prayer says, "Thy will (not mine) be done." We must never allow ourselves to be lulled into thinking we can play fast and loose and lose touch with the Lord with impunity. If we do, there's hell to pay!

Chapter 11

Young Elihu

(Job 32v1 – 36v21)

Eliphaz, Bildad and Zophar have finally given up on Job, realising they were getting nowhere. "He's too darned self-righteous," they all agreed. As ever their diagnosis was wide of the mark. They were actually the self-righteous ones. Job was truly righteous, inasmuch as he was the only one amongst them who had a meaningful personal relationship with the Lord. The others thought they knew all there was to know about God, but had never developed any kind of an intimate one on one relationship with Him. The very idea of doing so would have probably shocked them. God was to be observed from a respectful distance. If you tried to get too close it would surely be curtains.

At this point young Elihu turns up. He must have joined the gathering some time after the original three had arrived on the scene. He has obviously been quietly

listening to what has been said. Being a good deal
younger than the rest of the party, it would have been
frowned upon for him to have interrupted whilst the
others were having their say. But he was none too pleased
with what he had heard.

Job claimed to be blameless and could see no
justification for all the punishment that had been meted
out to him. Baldly put, he was implying that God was
acting unfairly; whereas his three friends for their part had
found no way to refute what he had said. In fact they had
all ended up arguing around in circles.

So Elihu now wades in with all guns blazing. "They say
the older you are, the wiser you become. I have to tell you,
I've listened carefully but I haven't heard much wisdom
from any of you! The truth is, it is the spirit of God in a
man, irrespective of age, that gives him understanding."

Elihu certainly isn't afraid of calling a spade a spade, or
showing disrespect to his elders whom he clearly does not
regard as his betters. "Tell me, Uncle Job, do you really
believe you are totally pure and without sin in God's
sight? Is it right that you should be complaining that He
has found fault with you and no longer talks to you? Let
me tell you, God never stops talking to each and everyone
of us – now one way – now another – though we may not
perceive it. He speaks to us in our dreams, sending us
warnings. At other times, perhaps through sickness, a
man may reach out to the Lord and be ransomed, healed,

restored, forgiven and brought back into right relationship once more. It is His desire to redeem us whatever the cost, whatever the situation. God does all these things time and time again to save us from hellfire and damnation, and bring us into the light of His presence.

"Come now, Uncle, hear me out. I will teach you some real wisdom." This youngster, Elihu, is pretty self-assured – even a bit full of himself, if you ask me. But let's not judge him too hastily. He may surprise us with what he's got to say.

"You claim you are innocent, but God is denying you justice. You consider yourself honest and upright, but for some inexplicable reason you are being made to look like a liar. You ask what is the point in trying to please God when things turn out the way they have for you?

"Listen to me, you great men of understanding! I think we can all agree that for God to be God it is impossible for Him to do wrong or for that matter to be unjust. After all He is the judge of all men, and His scales of justice set the standard. He is completely impartial as between rich and poor or strong and weak. Whoever we are, He is our Maker. He knows our every step. There is no need for any interrogation when we come before His judgment seat. We can make no pleas in mitigation. He knows the truth. – in fact He is the Truth!

"If we confess that we have sinned, repent and promise to mend our ways, should God reward us and pat us on the back for doing what we ought to have been doing all along anyway? Uncle Job, you seem to think God owes you one, because you've been such a good fellow. I've got news for you; God is no one's debtor. On the contrary, everything we have belongs to Him – even the very breath in our nostrils. If He withdrew His spirit from the world all mankind would perish. Despite all this, you have the temerity to accuse Him of not giving you a fair deal!

"Wisdom starts from God's perspective, not from our limited and biased angle. When we encounter adversity and affliction, don't blame God, but earnestly seek Him and call on Him to show you the way through. He never desires the death of a sinner, but would much rather he turned from his wickedness and lived.

"Uncle Job, you are in danger of impugning God's integrity. That would certainly not be wise. You have even called into question whether there is any personal advantage to be had in not sinning. Just think a moment what you are saying. Surely the question should be, 'What possible advantage does God derive from your not sinning?' It is impossible for God, by His very nature, to gain or lose anything by our being good or bad. Our wickedness or goodness affects only us and those around us. Our Maker, Creator and Teacher has shown us the way to go specifically for our own good and peace of mind, not His!

"If we care to ignore it and go our own sweet way

because of pride and pig-headedness, and then when in trouble cry out to Him for help, don't be surprised if He doesn't answer. If you turn your back on Him, He will turn His back on you.

"Uncle Job, you say your case is before Him, and all you can now do is wait for Him to explain Himself. You claim He takes no notice of the wickedness going on all around, but seems to have singled you out for unfair punishment. Who do you think you are to be standing in judgment on God?

"Just bear with me a little longer and hopefully I will be able to show you the error of your ways. Although God is omnipotent, He is ever mindful of us and always has our best interests at heart – hard though this may be for you to swallow at this point in time. You see, God's view of our best interests and our view of our best interests rarely coincide.

"Never fear, He does not take His eyes off the righteous for one moment. But if discipline, correction or testing is appropriate that is what will be handed out. Those that respond positively will come through with flying colours and be blessed. Those that don't, won't. They will harbour resentment in their hearts, and will refuse to turn to God for help even when all hell breaks loose in their lives." To paraphrase what Revelation 22v11 says, "Those who are living in sin will simply go on doing so willy-nilly, irrespective of God's warnings."

Elihu is now working up a good head of steam as he continues, "He is forever wooing us to come out of whatever bondage has ensnared us, to experience the freedom and security that comes from a life totally committed to Him. That, my dear Uncle, is the personal advantage to be had from a righteous life. Don't let substitutes fool you – like riches and power and selfish ambition. They are not to be compared with the wisdom, understanding and joy you get from knowing and serving the Lord."

Young Elihu is really preaching up quite a storm. The point he is making is that humanity, in its self-centred and self-interested fashion, always approaches discussions about the whys and wherefores of God from the wrong end of the stick. We need to start with God and not ourselves; just like Genesis 1v1 puts it, "In the beginning God….." This is impossible without godly wisdom. Where is such wisdom found? Only with the Lord, of course! And how do we acquire it? By prayer and meditation in the scriptures – in essence, by spending time with Him. He is the only source of supply, but I am happy to relate that supplies are unlimited to those who are genuinely seeking. As Jesus explained in the Gospels, "Ask and it will be given you; seek and you will find; knock and the door will be opened to you."

Chapter 12

God Inhabits The Praises
Of His People

(Job 36v22 – 37v24)

I have taken the liberty of having Elihu address Job as 'uncle'. You will recall in chapter 1, when identifying who all the characters were, we discovered that Elihu was Job's first cousin twice removed. This means he was junior to Job by two generations and could quite easily have been about fifty years younger. For instance, if Job was, for the sake of argument, eighty, then Elihu could have been only thirty. In the circumstances it seems likely that a family relative this much younger would indeed address his elder cousin as 'uncle'.

Having upbraided his uncle in no uncertain terms for questioning God's motives in delivering or withholding justice as the case may be, he now launches forth into what could best be described as a hymn of praise in celebration of God's greatness, power, might, dominion and majesty –

a sort of 'halleluia chorus'. As we discovered earlier, Elihu was a member of the tribe of Judah, which means 'praise' in Hebrew. So what could be more natural! During the course of this exaltation a thunderstorm breaks out, ushering in the Lord Himself, which very definitely stops them all in their tracks! But let's not get ahead of ourselves.

It is worth noting that praise and worship is here, and elsewhere throughout the Bible, the means used for entering into the presence of God. This should be no surprise, for scripture does tell us that the Lord inhabits the praises of His people. If we are seriously determined to come into His presence then there is no better way than with singing and rejoicing before Him, and exuberantly expressing ourselves in worship.

I have always found community singing particularly stirring. Occasions that come to mind are the Last Night of the Proms with the audience and the massed choirs all joining in the singing of Rule Britannia, and the hymn 'Abide with Me' sung by 100,000 spectators at the old Wembley Stadium soccer Cup Finals. Neither of these is actually a Christian gathering as such, but the principle is the same. A spirit of unity envelops one and somehow the whole becomes greater than the sum of its parts.

In Revelation 5vv11-13 we read, "Then I looked and heard the voice of many angels, numbering thousands upon thousands, and ten thousand times ten thousand.

They encircled the Throne and …….. in a loud voice they sang: 'Worthy is the Lamb who was slain, to receive power and wealth and wisdom and strength and honour and glory and praise!'

"Then I heard every creature in heaven and on earth and under the earth and on the seas, and all that is in them, singing: 'To Him who sits on the Throne and to the Lamb be praise and honour and glory and power, for ever and ever!" By all accounts it is going to be kind of noisy up there. In the meantime, in preparation for that great and glorious day, we would do well to join in a few choir practices whilst down here on earth.

It is surely a godly thing to be stirred by songs of praise. Likewise, the blending of hearts, minds and voices in unity to worship the Lord, I am convinced, stirs the heart of God. For He has promised, that when we gather together for this purpose, He will be there in our midst.

Now Elihu opens his heart and mouth in praise and adoration.

"Our God is exalted in power and might;
He dwells in the realms of celestial light.
There is no teacher as wise as He;
There's none but God makes the blind to see.
He's flawless and faultless, His judgments are true;
He alone deserves praise as His justly due.
We have all seen it and gazed from afar,
How great and how glorious You really are.

You are forever the Ancient of Days

The only One worthy of worship and praise."

(Job 36vv22-26)

With the gathering thunderstorm come the first drops of rain, then the wind picks up and the heavens open, so to speak! Now the thunder is heard and lightning bolts flash overhead. "Praise the Lord!" shouts Elihu over the clamour, "Look at the power of the Almighty. Who can doubt that He is the one who ultimately governs the nations. He sends the rain and provides food for the hungry. Listen, listen! Do you hear that thunder? That's like the roar of His voice. Our God has done great things, way beyond our wildest imaginings. When He has a mind to bless He throws open the floodgates of heaven. He is abundant and holds nothing back. We stand amazed at the work of His hands. The very wind and waves obey Him."

Doesn't this remind you of Jesus when He and His disciples went sailing off across Lake Galilee and ran into a furious squall? Those stout fishermen were in fear of their lives until Jesus stood up in the back of the boat and rebuked the wind and said to the waves, "Hush, be still!" Then the wind died down and it was completely calm. The disciples were terrified at this demonstration of divine power and said, "Heavens above! Who the deuce is this bloke, that even the wind and the waves obey him?" Having in all likelihood had the Book of Job read to them in the Synagogue, the penny was probably slowly beginning to drop.

It makes you wonder. For all our modern day hi-tec expertise, for all the billions spent on sending satellites hither and yon, for all the scientific research with instruments of unbelievable precision and accuracy, we are still unable to control the weather, have no idea where the next earthquake will occur and only the vaguest notion of when another volcano is likely to erupt. We can put men on the moon, we send probes into outer space and pronounce authoritatively on "black holes" and how the universe is supposed to have begun billions of years ago with a "big bang"; and yet these so-called scientific boffins can't tell us with any certainty whether it is going to be a nice day to go on a picnic next Saturday!

"Dear Uncle Job, stop and consider God's wonders. Have you any idea how He controls the weather? How He makes heat waves here and produces hurricanes and tempests there? Why He blesses one with sunshine and showers and punishes another with blizzards and floods? Can you be really serious when you say you want to present Him with a petition? What should we, or could we say? Be reasonable! You can't honestly be wanting to meet with God face to face. You'd be swallowed up. You can't look at the sun for more than a moment without damaging your eyes. God is a million times brighter. His splendour is awesome, nonetheless for all His exalted majesty He reaches down from the highest heights and cares for the oppressed and downtrodden, but assuredly has no regard for the worldly wise or proud. He refreshes the weary and gives power to the weak. Those that hope in the Lord will renew their strength. They will soar on wings like eagles. That is why we revere and reverence Him."

That's some encomium! - and sure enough like all genuine praise and worship sessions God turns up and starts speaking to Job in the midst of the storm.

Chapter 13

The Lord Speaks

(Job 38v1 – 40v5)

The Lord turns up and stops everyone in their tracks. When He sweeps onto the scene, talk about 'shock and awe', they are literally gobsmacked. It seems the rumblings of thunder from the storm have miraculously turned into the very words of God as they listen fearfully to what He has to say. He addresses Himself almost exclusively to Job.

The desire of Job's heart over the past few chapters has been to be granted an interview with God. It is worth remembering that nothing pleases our Father in heaven more than to give us the desires of our heart when they are in accordance with His will, so perhaps we sometimes need to think twice before making our requests known to Him. We may get more than we bargained for! He is able to do immeasurably more than all we ask or imagine according to His power that is at work within us, as St

Paul tells us in Ephesians 3v20.

The Lord Almighty is about to speak. What on earth is He likely to say? No doubt He has heard every word they have been batting back and forth in their feeble attempts to try and explain God and the workings of His mind. Now that He has actually deigned to grace the proceedings with His presence, they must all be feeling just a trifle foolish.

Try and put yourself in their place. I think they'd either want to run and hide or else prostrate themselves in abject obeisance. The truth of the matter is, godliness in its purest form, and you can't get a much purer form than God Himself, is an awesome and terrifying experience for your average ho-humdrummer, let alone a bunch of old Middle Eastern sheiks!

If there is one thing I have learnt about God, there are no brownie points to be earned in trying to second guess Him. He is a lateral thinker to end all lateral thinking. You expect the answer to your prayer to come one way, and lo and behold it comes another. Very often things one originally thought were curses turn out to be blessings in disguise. We always need to approach Him with an open mind and an open heart. Otherwise we may find ourselves missing the message, and missing the boat entirely.

When Moses asked God to reveal Himself to him in all His glory, without probably quite realising the enormity of what he was asking, the Lord graciously agreed and said,

"I will cause my goodness to pass in front of you and I
will proclaim my Name in your presence." Then as Moses,
completely overawed, bows down and worships, the Lord
goes by, wrapped in what the Jews call the shekinah, which
is a Hebrew word denoting the indefinable glory of God's
presence. This is similar to what Peter, James and John
experienced on the Mount of Transfiguration when Jesus
was suddenly enveloped in a cloud of dazzling brightness
and they heard a voice saying, "This is my Son, whom I
love. Mark well what He tells you."

I have often wondered why it was so important for God
to proclaim His Name. Therein lies one of the
profoundest mysteries of the Judeo-Christian faith. We
are told throughout scripture to do everything 'in the
Name of the Lord' or 'in the Name of Jesus'. When we
pray we invariably end our prayers in this way. Why? It
is to remind us that it is only 'in Him' that we live and
move and have our being. We have no standing or right to
be heard 'outside His Name'. As Jesus so succinctly put it,
"I am the Way, the Truth and the Life, no one comes to the
Father but by me." It is His will we are all called to
submit to and live by. It is His will we interminably pray
to be done here on earth, as it is already being done in
heaven.

When Moses first encountered God at the burning bush
and asked His Name the Bible tells us he got the enigmatic
reply, **"I AM THAT I AM."** What kind of a name is

that? In fact what God uttered initially was the unpronounceable Hebrew tetragrammaton, "YHWH", which can best be described as a deep exhalation of breath – the Spirit of the Lord. Breathe on me breath of God! You will doubtless recall that Jesus after His resurrection, breathed on the disciples saying, "Receive the Holy Spirit." The original YHWH has now been given vowels and is transliterated in our Bibles as either Jehovah or Yahweh.

So with Moses lying prostrate as God's shekinah majestically breezes by, what is He now going to proclaim His Name to be? YHWH naturally. As He passes in front of Moses, He sighs deeply, "YHWH, YHWH – the compassionate and gracious God, slow to anger, abounding in love and faithfulness, maintaining love to thousands, and forgiving wickedness, rebellion and sin. Yet He does not leave the guilty unpunished."

A person's name in the Hebrew tradition is very often descriptive of the character. Take Abraham for instance. He started life as Abram – 'exalted elder' – until God changed it to 'patriarch of a multitude', and made him the founder of the Israeli nation.

Likewise, Jacob, his grandson, means 'cheat, usurper and one who is forever living by his own cunning and craftiness'. This describes the early part of Jacob's life to a tee. He outwitted his elder twin brother, Esau, into relinquishing his claim to be the elder of the two, and then shamelessly colluded with his mother in deceiving his blind old father in order to steal the patriarchal blessing that was rightfully Esau's. What a scoundrel! He then has to flee to avoid being murdered by his brother.

His mother packs Jacob off to her brother, Laban, another artful dodger. There he spends the next twenty years pitting his wits and cunning against his uncle and very definitely living in his own strength. It is not until he decides to return to Canaan, the land of promise, and face his brother once more that he at last realizes how inadequate his own shiftiness is in the face of the test now confronting him. In the past, by dint of his own wit and will, he had always managed to get by. God now brings him to a place where only total reliance on the Almighty will suffice. The Lord wrestles with him all night eventually bringing him to the point of surrender. At last he glimpses God for who He really is – the omnipotent, all-sufficient one. It is then that he is re-named, Israel – 'God rules'.

The experiences of Job and Jacob have certain similarities. Job was prepared to grapple with his friends and maintain his point against all their arguments until, through the intervention of Elihu, God turns up and starts 'wrestling' with him. He comes down upon him directly with all the majesty of His power, overwhelms him by the display of His greatness and glory and elicits from him the famous admission, "My ears had heard of You, but now my eyes have seen You. Therefore I despise myself and repent in dust and ashes." Nothing but a full revelation of who God is can really lead to genuine repentance and true humility. Only then do things come into right perspective. It is only then we understand that the vastness of the divide between Him and us can be bridged by no one else but Jesus Christ. Our own puny good works, self-righteousness and the like, pale into insignificance by comparison.

I have laboured this point somewhat because the occasions when God turns up and engages in face to face conversation are, biblically speaking, not that frequent. Generally His messages are conveyed by angels or prophets or through meditating in His Word. Job is about to experience something pretty special. Direct consultations with the Lord God Almighty are not exactly run-of-the-mill everyday stuff! It would be, at one and the same time, both terrifying and exhilaratingly uplifting.

The thunder rolls and God's voice booms in upon Job's consciousness.

"Who do you think you are, trying to tell Me how to behave? Do you really believe you have more knowledge than I? Stand up like a man. If you're so clever I'm sure you won't mind answering a few questions.

"Where were you when the earth was created? Do you remember the song the stars were singing, when all the angels were shouting for joy? Who gave the waves of the sea their boundaries, and told them, 'Thus far and no further'? Who set the seasons and the times for dawn and dusk? Have you seen the gates of hell, and do you know all there is to know about the vast expanses of the earth? Where do light and darkness come from?

"Come, come now, Job, surely you have the answers? You're so old and wise and have been around for such ages, how can you not know these things?"

The Lord almost seems to be teasing Job. Actually He is setting the stage to make some seriously important points and give Job and all of us fascinating insights into His way of looking at things.

"How about hail and snow? Where do they come from? Or for that matter, lightning, storm and tempest, or frost and ice? Do you understand the movements of the stars and constellations and the eternal laws that govern the universe? Or even the divine laws that govern the earth?"

This is like an A level exam in astronomy, physics and a bit of meteorology thrown in for good measure! Interestingly, through scientific research we, today, can answer many of these questions, perhaps not comprehensively, but at least in part. To Job and his buddies 3,500 years ago this would have been way beyond their ken. The next exam papers are in philosophy, psychology and natural history.

"Where does wisdom come from? Who devised the mechanism that enables the mind to understand? Who has the responsibility for seeing that the rain falls in due season and even the remotest parts are tended and cared for? Who looks after the wild animals in the jungle and provides food for the birds? What do you know about the mating habits of mountain goats and how their young are born? Can you tell me about the wild donkey and how he spends his days in the hills? Can you tame the wild ox and get him to till your land?

"What do you know about the ostrich? She is a stupid creature, because I made her that way, but boy can she run! And how about the horse? Fast and strong and eager to dash into the fray at the blast of the bugle, - who made him that way? Is it your skill that enables the hawk to take flight? Can you teach the eagle how to soar in the heights and build his eyrie on the mountaintop?

"Come now, Job, how long do you need to answer these questions? Aren't you the one who claimed to have a bone to pick with Me? Didn't I hear you say that you thought I'd got it wrong? Well, if you have all the answers, then I suppose it might just be possible that you know more than I do. Otherwise I suggest you accept that I know best."

When I was sitting my accountancy exam finals, they were held in a large municipal building in London where many other exams were being sat at the same time in adjacent halls. We filed in and dutifully took our places at the desks with the exam paper face down in front of us, awaiting the invigilator's command to turn the paper over and start writing. Within minutes of the signal being given, the fellow sitting next to me slowly and solemnly rose to his feet and fell flat on his face in a dead faint. He was, it transpired, a medical student who had a panic attack when he realised he was in the wrong exam hall! I mention this strange episode because by now poor old Job must have been feeling much the same.

He is covered in confusion and embarrassment. "I am lost for words. There's no way I could possibly answer your questions. It was foolish of me to imagine I could ever take issue with you on anything. Now I see how truly great you are I am speechless."

We would all do well to learn the lesson Job learnt. Contending with God is a no-brainer. If there is something about Him we don't like or can't make sense of, we need to start from the premise that God is always in the right, and any difficulty in coming to grips with the problem lies on our side of the fence. This is why it is so necessary to pray constantly for His wisdom, understanding and insight to see the situation from His perspective.

Chapter 14

Dinosaurs and Dragons

(Job 40v6 – 41v34)

The Lord continues to speak to Job out of the thunderstorm.

"Job, stop grovelling. Stand up like a man, I haven't finished with you yet. I have some more questions and I insist you answer me."

Poor Job! He must be quaking in his boots wondering what's coming next. He's probably wishing he'd let sleeping dogs lie, and was back whingeing quietly to himself in his wretched ashpit. Having aroused God he's having to face a good deal more music than he had bargained for. But it has to be said that Job is the kind of person God cares to do business with. Job was desperate for answers and he wasn't about to give up until he had them. This is not unlike the parable Jesus told of the importunate widow in Luke 18.

In a certain town there was a crooked judge who didn't

give a fig for dispensing proper justice. There was also a widow woman who kept pestering him with her plea for a court order against her adversary. He kept on postponing his decision, hoping she'd drop her case and go away. He really didn't want to be bothered. But she kept on at him refusing to take no for an answer, until he couldn't stand it any longer. He said, "If she carries on this way she'll wear me out." So, in exasperation, he let her have the court order just to get rid of her.

Then Jesus said, "If a crooked, lazy judge will do this for an old widow woman, how much quicker do you think the just and righteous Judge of the universe will answer the pleas of those who cry out to Him day and night? I tell you He will see to it they get justice and speedily."

Those who persist and persevere in prayer, banging away on the door of heaven, are the ones who most often get the results.

So, what was God's next question?

"From what I heard of your discussion with your friends, it sounded to me very much as if you were trying to discredit Me to justify yourself. Did you not say that your heart was pure and therefore it was unjust of Me to have put you through the wringer like this? Who are you to judge what is right or wrong?"

Let's face it, if God thinks our faith needs to be tested, then so be it. Everyone's faith needs testing from time to time. Just because we may be brilliant students doesn't exempt us from periodic examination. On the contrary, it is testing that validates and gives accreditation to our progress, and gives us the confidence to move onto higher grades. In fact it's as a result of the constant tests and trials that we become stronger and more mature as Christians.

God continues His inquisition. "How far can your arms reach? To the stars? How far can your voice carry? To the ends of the earth? `If so, then clothe yourself in honour and majesty. Bring down the proud and crush the wicked, and I will be the first to admit that you are able to save yourself. In that case you need no saviour."

The implication here is clear. If you can't do any of these things – and, let's face it, who can except God – then you cannot save yourself in this world. We all need a saviour.

This is where the karma religions, such as Hinduism, Buddhism and Jainism, all fall down. You can never amass enough credits in this life to earn salvation. We can do good deeds in our own strength till we're blue in the face, but in the final analysis Isaiah tells us they amount to no more than a pile of filthy rags in God's sight. Not until we are saved – and there is salvation in no other name but Jesus - and doing all as unto God, will good works start yielding eternal benefits.

Now comes the really fascinating bit about dinosaurs and dragons.

"Consider the behemoth dinosaur," says God, "which I created on the sixth day along with all the other animals and Adam and Eve as well for that matter. He eats grass like the cattle, but what strength, what power! He has a swaying tail as thick and long as a tall tree trunk. His bones and limbs are like pillars. He is the greatest beast I made. Despite his fearsome proportions he is not fierce. As he lies amongst the marsh reeds the wild animals safely roam nearby. Nothing alarms him, he is big enough to overcome all dangers. But don't try catching him, you'll find him too strong by half."

Isn't that interesting? My Bible has a margin note saying, 'possibly the hippopotamus or the elephant'. I don't think so. Have you noticed the tail on either of these beasts? It is certainly nothing like a tree trunk! But in truth this is a pretty fair description of a diplodocus or one or other of that species of dinosaur. Evolutionists tell us dinosaurs were roaming the earth millions of years ago – long before mankind came on the scene. Here God states that they were created at the same time as the rest of us. I am inclined to believe God rather than a load of largely atheistic evolutionists.

What next?

"Let me tell you about the leviathan. You certainly can't pull this monster out of the sea with a fishing rod or slip a bit and bridle on him. You'll make no pet of such a creature and you will never be able to lead him meekly to market. If you so much as lay a finger on him you'll remember the struggle to your dying day, and you won't want to be doing it again. There's absolutely no way you can overpower him. The sight of him is enough to terrify anyone. And I created him! Who then can possibly stand up against Me? Who has a claim against Me that I must repay? Everything in the universe and upon the earth is Mine. I am the inventor, the creator, the author and the finisher. Nothing begins or ends without Me.

"Let me tell you more about this leviathan sea-dragon." Again, a margin note tells me, 'possibly the crocodile'. Once again, I don't think so. This fellow is rather special as we shall soon discover. "He is large-limbed and graceful in form with a protective armour coating. Like the behemoth you would be foolish to try and approach him with a bridle. As for his mouth, you really wouldn't want to look inside at his razor-sharp teeth. His back is covered with rows of impenetrable thick horn-like scales." Thus far I guess the description could fit a crocodile or even a stegosaurus or some such. But now comes something to really blow your mind! – and don't forget this is God speaking, not some spinning politician. "His snorting throws out flames, his eyes flash like the rising sun, fire and sparks shoot out from his mouth and smoke pours from his nostrils. His breath sets coals ablaze."

Can you believe it! Why not? There are tales galore in mythology about fire-breathing dragons. Maybe these myths are not so mythical after all and are actually based on prehistoric fact. Palaeontology has established that certain primeval specimens may well have had this idiosyncrasy. Even today there are fireflies which can self-generate electricity. So, you see, it is not so unbelievable. It may well have been these verses that gave Tolkien the idea for Smaug, the dreadful dragon in The Hobbit. As if what has been described already were not enough, God has still more to tell us about this frightening creature.

"There is amazing strength in his neck and all are scared witless when he approaches. His chest is as hard as rock and when he rises up on his hind legs even the brave are terrified. As he thrashes about they run for their lives. No sword, spear or javelin makes the slightest impression on him. Slingstones are as dust and a club no more than a piece of straw. He laughs at man's feeble efforts to subdue him. He makes the sea churn like a boiling cauldron and leaves a glistening white wake behind as he speeds off into the deep. There is nothing on earth quite like him – completely fearless. One encounter with him and even the proud and haughty are put in their place."

Some say that this was the serpent that beguiled Eve in the Garden of Eden. If Eve had come face to face with this beast I rather think she might have lost her appetite! Nonetheless, I firmly believe that this is a fair description by God of one of the creatures of His original creation – now mercifully extinct!

This whole narrative puts into perspective the vastness of the divide there is between us and God. We do well to constantly bear this in mind when through His grace and mercy He invites us to enter into an intimate personal relationship with Him. It is not a relationship of equals. In these democratic times we tend to think of all men as equal and God in much the same way. That is a big mistake. Getting too familiar inhibits true worship. We are to revere and reverence Him and endeavour to become more and more like Him.

This reminds me of football fans. They idolise their club, be it Manchester United or the like, and their star players. If David Beckham gets a special haircut, then many of his fans do too. If he has an earring, so do they. They read his book, they wear the T-shirt. They spend a small fortune on season tickets and following their team around the world.

As Christians we should behave similarly. If Jesus fed the hungry, so should we. If He healed the sick, so should we, and we should certainly be reading His book. How sacrificial and fanatical is our Christianity? Those football fans can perhaps teach us a thing or two about spending generously doing what really turns them on. It's all very well going to church and worshipping and idolising the Lord, but what is it costing us? King David said, "I will not make sacrifices to the Lord that cost me nothing." Neither should we. If a mere game like soccer can elicit such extravagant devotion from its supporters, how much more should a life and death matter like following Jesus do so!   Like the football fans we need to be eating, sleeping and breathing our faith in Christ.

Chapter 15

The End Of The Matter

(Job 42)

Having listened intently to the astounding things the Lord had been telling him, Job capitulates and acknowledges that God's thoughts are way above his. "I had heard that you were glorious and majestic, but now that you have spoken I realise I never understood the half of it. I see that you can do all things. No plan of yours could possibly ever fail. You asked, 'Who is this that presumes to boast about his knowledge in my presence?' I'm sorry I ever opened my mouth. Truly you are the fount of all wisdom and the embodiment of things that are altogether too wonderful and mysterious for me to know."

What Job says here reminds me of St Paul's comment in 2 Corinthians 12. He talks about being caught up to paradise and there hearing inexpressible things that man is not permitted to tell. No words can describe the wonders that God has in store for those that sincerely love Him. The odd spot of bother in this world, or even Job-sized calamities, are not to be compared to the glories that await the redeemed of the Lord; as Paul puts it in 1 Corinthians 2v9: "No eye has seen, nor ear has heard, no mind has conceived what God has prepared for those who love Him." That was way back then. Now, with the advantage of 'anno domini', God has revealed it to us by His Holy Spirit, albeit through a glass darkly.

I think many Christians today would do well to adjust their focus and see the Lord for who He really is. Oftentimes the image we have of God is too small to some and too remote to others. It's as if we were looking through the wrong end of a telescope. The Bible exhorts us to magnify Him, and constantly remind ourselves of how great He is, and that He is here with us all the time even though we don't always perceive it.

Job continues to make his apologies. "You said, 'Listen now, and I will speak; I will question you, and you shall answer me.' My ears had heard of you, but now my eyes have seen you. What can I do but humble myself and repent in dust and ashes!" This reflects what scripture tells us in 2 Chronicles 7v14: 'If my people who are called by my name, will humble themselves and pray, and seek my face and turn from their wicked ways, then will I hear from heaven and will forgive their sin and will heal their land.'

The Lord now turns on the three comforters. "I am angry with you three, because you totally misrepresented Me to Job. I am YHWH – the compassionate and gracious One, slow to anger, abounding in love and faithfulness, maintaining love to thousands, and forgiving wickedness, rebellion and sin. Now go and make a sacrifice to purify yourselves and ask Job to pray and intercede for you, so that you will not suffer for your folly."

That sorted out Eliphaz, Zophar and Bildad double quick. Before you could say 'knife' they'd made their sacrifices, and were begging Job to pray for them. If I'd been him, after all they'd said, I would have been tempted to let them stew in their own juice a while. But Job was righteous and upright – remember – so he prayed and the Lord heard and relented.

It's fortunate for all of us that God is in the forgiveness business. When Jonah, of whale belly fame, was called by God to go and warn the people of Nineveh that unless they repented they would all be destroyed, he didn't much fancy the assignment and set off in the opposite direction. After some hair raising experiences on and under the high seas he stops fooling about and gets on with the job God has given him. He preaches so effectively to the Ninevites that they actually do all repent. So God relents and disaster is averted. Jonah was none too thrilled. He didn't much care for the Assyrians in the first place. They weren't exactly God's chosen people. What's more, he was a prophet who had just predicted they were all about to be wiped out. As a prophet, it looks bad on your CV if your predictions don't come to pass. So Jonah sulked, until God pointed out that He was deeply concerned for all mankind, in which case so too should we be. His mercy extends to all who will humble themselves and turn to Him in sincerity and faith.

After Job had prayed for his friends, the Lord made him prosperous again. In fact He gave him twice as much as he'd had before. You will recall in chapter 2 we discovered he was at that time multi-mega-rich. Now he's super-multi-mega-rich! All the ships he thought had been wrecked on the rocks and had foundered in a storm suddenly came in laden down with goodies. He was back in business big time! Job had shown himself faithful despite the terrible things he had had to endure. God honours that. Scripture tells us that He enjoys being exceedingly abundantly generous to those who genuinely acknowledge Him as their Lord and Saviour. Testing times will occur, but provided we cling to Him, He will always see us through the valley of the shadow of death and we can live as overcomers. "In all these things we are more than conquerors through Him who loved us." *(Rom 8v37)*

It's true that life sometimes does not seem to be fair. I have friends who have had the most devastating experiences. In these circumstances it is tempting to shake one's fist at God and cry out, "Why do you allow such terrible things to happen? If you truly loved us, you'd protect us from such disasters." God has created a chance-ridden environment to develop our characters and test our integrity. Every day of our life that we are fortunate enough to see we need to be eternally grateful to God for the opportunity this gives us to love and serve both Him and His creation.

Obviously Job has recovered from his ghastly illness and all his old friends and family come visiting once more. They commiserate with him over all he has had to suffer and bring him gifts and all sorts. In fact he's having quite a party! He is again honoured and respected as a great chief amongst his clan. It is almost as if God were sorry for what He had allowed to happen and was at pains to compensate Job fully for all the trouble he had been put to.

"How many sheep did you lose?" asks the Lord, "7,000 you say? Well here are 14,000 by way of replacement. You also had 3,000 camels, 1,000 oxen and 500 donkeys? Alright then, will you settle for twice that number? Job, I want to bless you like you've never been blessed before. You've been through a real grilling, but I can see you are a man after my own heart. Well done, my good and faithful servant. Enter now into the joy of your Lord." This is just like the scriptures in Malachi 3v10 and Luke 6v38 tell us that if we will only honour God, it is His good pleasure to pour down abundant blessings upon us.

Then Job, somewhat emboldened by God's

overwhelming generosity, says, "By the way, have you forgotten the children I lost – all seven sons and three daughters? I now have no heirs. To be honest, I feel their loss much more keenly than all the rest of the stuff that was taken from me."

"Of course you do," says the Lord, "I will see to it you have seven more sons and three more lovely daughters. They will be the most beautiful girls in all the land." I'm not too sure what Job's wife may have thought of this part of the blessing. "Oh no, not another ten children to give birth to and bring up at my time of life!" Considering her earlier comment about cursing God and dropping dead, it is probable that she was no longer the mother superior in the Job household and had been traded in for a more recent model! What's more, Leviticus 24 tells us that anyone who curses God must be put to death. So she may well not have been around when the munificence was being poured out.

Another point worth observing here is that, although he was compensated with double all his chattels, Job only received the same number of sons and daughters he had lost. Why do you suppose this was? The human spirit never dies. Therefore, by having seven more sons and three more daughters he was effectively getting double. It also suggests that the first bunch, contrary to what Zophar had intimated, were already waiting to be reunited with him in heaven.

Oddly, we are told the names of Job's three daughters, Jemimah, Keziah, and Keren-Happuch, but no mention is made of the boys. Scripture also states that Job granted the girls an inheritance along with their brothers. This would have been most unusual in his day and age. Clearly there was no gender discrimination in his household. In God's economy blessings apply equally and without partiality to both male and female alike. Functions and responsibilities will differ, but all, irrespective of who, are invited to enjoy God's blessings of salvation and a rich and rewarding life in Jesus Christ. Then, like Job, we also can live happily ever after - in the hereafter!

Epilogue

The Book of Job teaches us that life here on earth is a training ground. It's a lesson in response and responsibility. How responsive are we to God? How aware are we of God's presence in our lives every minute of every day, not just for an hour or so on Sundays? Do we truly realize how lost we are without His guidance, and how precarious life can be? He is indeed our life-raft to which we need to cling for all we are worth, for it is only in Him we live and move and have our being. Without Him we wallow around out of our depth and easy prey for the sharks of this world.

But just as we are to be responsive to God, we are equally responsible for heeding His call and going and doing His will here on earth as it is done in heaven. You are probably now asking, "And what might this be?" Simply stated, it is to receive God's love into our hearts unreservedly, and then pass it on self-sacrificially to all and sundry with whom we come in contact day by day. This is the good news Jesus came to tell us. This is not sloppy, emotional, passive sentimentalism. It is powerful, active and energetic because it is energised by God's Holy Spirit; besides which it is also gracious, compassionate, merciful and forgiving because it flows from the heart of God.

We mere human beings could never in a month of Sundays manage this in our own strength. It is only with God's Spirit in our hearts that we can aspire to such heights. It is only then that we will soar on wings as eagles and be seated in heavenly places with Christ Jesus, and be able to view all things from God's perspective and apply true godly wisdom to the problems here on earth.

In Luke 13 Jesus makes a very telling observation on a couple of topical events which would have certainly made the front page of the local tabloids. Some Galileans who were quietly minding their own business and had been ritually sacrificing an animal or two in the performance of their religious observances, for no particular reason fell foul of a squad of Pilate's soldiers and were promptly massacred and left for dead along with the animals they had just been slaughtering. Perhaps the soldiers were vegetarians or anti blood sports. No reason is given for this wanton killing. Out of the blue it just happened.

Likewise, at about the same time a tower in Siloam mysteriously collapsed killing eighteen unlucky bystanders. Again no reason is given for this tragic accident. Jesus merely says, "Do you think these folk were worse sinners than all the rest of you, and they simply got their just deserts? No way! I tell you, terrible things like these are going to happen from time to time. Life is like that. You never know the hour you will be called to meet your Maker. So be sure you have repented and accepted the Lord as your Saviour, then sudden disaster need hold no terrors for you. Otherwise be prepared to meet a fate worse than death." Jesus was not one to mince His words. He told it like it is and we would be well advised to heed the warning.

Can we say with Job, "I know that my redeemer lives, and that in the end He will stand upon the earth; and after my body has been destroyed, yet in my flesh I will see God"? That's the faith that saw Job through his trials, and that's the faith that will see each one of us through this life whatever the world, the flesh or the devil may throw at us. This is the faith that enables us at the last to stand blameless before God. Perhaps 'blameless' in this context could be rephrased 'be lameless' and cease limping around in a half-hearted, double-minded, lame-brained manner. We need to stand tall and, as the song says, be 'forthright, outright, downright, upright' and declare unequivocally like Joshua, "As for me and my household, we will serve the Lord, come what may."

Now in the words of Jude 24-25: "To Him who is able to keep you from falling and to present you before His glorious presence without fault (and blameless) and with great joy – to the only wise God, our Saviour, be glory, majesty, power and authority, through Jesus Christ, our Lord, before all ages, now and forevermore! Amen."